THE FEDERAL DEFICIT

Fiscal Imprudence or Policy Weapon?

Edited with an introduction by
WILLIAM HAMOVITCH
QUEENS COLLEGE

D. C. HEATH AND COMPANY · BOSTON

CONTENTS

iii

IV. BUSINESS OPPOSITION TO DEFICIT SPENDING

V. THE ROLE OF FEDERAL DEFICITS: THE EMPIRICAL RECORD

INTRODUCTION

The 1930's saw a sharp change in thinking about much of economic theory and policy and nowhere is this more marked than in the area of fiscal policy. Some of the major changes in macro-economics used to be referred to as the Keynesian Revolution but are now widely accepted and integrated into the mainstream of economic thought.

The traditional fiscal view prior to the 1930's included the proposition that government budgets should be balanced annually. The major arguments of classical economists in favor of this principle are presented by Jesse Burkhead in the first selection of these readings. It will be seen that some of these economists were not completely rigid on this point and did allow for borrowing in such cases as financing war and large non-recurring productive capital projects. In general, though, budget balancing was a guiding rule. Little or no thought was given to the idea of using tax and expenditure policies for any kind of stabilization program. In part, this principle was supported on the ground that any allowance of deficits would lead to fiscal irresponsibility and excessive, wasteful expenditures. Further, for many, this view was predicated on the belief that there was a natural tendency toward stability and full employment of resources and hence no need for fiscal manipulations. For these two main reasons, the levying of taxes equal to expenditures was considered necessary to keep the latter to a minimum and to divert scarce resources from the private to the public sector of the economy. Under the full employment assumption, allowing expenditures to exceed taxes could lead to excessive demand and inflation as the government injected more spending into the system than it withdrew. In this view, balancing the budget not only leads to government prudence but also contributes to economic stability. Unbalanced budgets, by which is usually meant deficits, could only be unstabilizing and inflationary.

The onset of the great depression and the "New Economics," introduced by Keynes and others, altered this view of both the functioning of the economy and the role of fiscal policy. One of the major conclusions emanating from Keynesian doctrine was that it is incorrect to assume that a free private enterprise economy will automatically tend toward full, or reasonably full, utilization of resources. Instead, in Keynes' model, it is possible for the economy to be in equilibrium at any number of levels of income and employment, including levels considerably below full employment. To put the thesis another way, Keynes held that full employment is only one of many possible equilibrium positions.

Many economists who subscribed to this new doctrine, or variations of it, were led to a search for policies to achieve and maintain full employment. Some contended that nothing short of comprehensive government planning could achieve the desired goal. Others argued for more moderate selective controls; included among these was the suggestion of some that direct control of investment was needed because of its high degree of instability. These schemes for a large amount of government intervention in the economy did not win much support among either economists or the public at large, at least in the United States. However, the use of fiscal policy as a stabilizing device has come to be accepted, virtually unanimously by economists although admittedly less so by the general population. It is a form of indirect control in that it does not interfere directly in the decision-making processes of individuals and business firms.

The policy of economic stabilization has also been incorporated into a governmental responsibility through the passage of the Employment Act of 1946. This Act implicitly endorsed the use of fiscal policy as one measure which the government should use to try to achieve maximum employment, production, and purchasing power. The President has the obligation of presenting an annual report to Congress on economic conditions and outlook together with policy recommendations aimed at attaining the highest possible level of economic performance. The Act established the Council of Economic Advisers to aid the President in this task. In addition, the Joint Committee of the Economic Report in Congress was created to study the President's and other relevant economic reports and proposals and to make recommendations for improvement in the methods of implementing and harmonizing the economic policies of government.

In essence, the ideas inherent in the stabilizing function of fiscal policy are rather simple. If, from the viewpoint of economic performance, aggregate demand is either too high or too low, this can be remedied by compensatory fiscal action. If the level of demand is insufficient to achieve the desired level of output and employment, the government can adopt various combinations of tax and expenditure policies to bolster it. The simplest prescription would call for an increase in government expenditures for an immediate direct rise in spending and/or a decrease in taxes to increase private spending. In both cases there would be further increases in spending via the multiplier process, as people who received incomes would spend some portion of it, leading to a further rise of income, still more spending, and so on. In addition, there could be some pump-priming as businessmen might be induced to increase investment in response to higher consumer spending. If pump-priming worked with sufficient force, it would in time remove the need for continuing the original government fiscal action.

A consequence of the described policy would, at least in the short run, be a budget deficit, to be financed, ordinarily, by borrowing. If the full expansionary effect of the tax and/or expenditure policies is to be realized, the borrowing would have to be done in such a way as to preclude any adverse effect on consumption and investment. This could be accomplished if the government securities issued to finance the deficits were bought by commercial banks or from idle balances of individuals, corporations, and other institutions. A danger here is that the government borrowing, through its increase in demand for funds, might lead to a rise in interest rates with a possible adverse effect on investment. This could be obviated if the monetary authorities cooperate by providing the banking system with adequate reserves and the economy with sufficient liquidity to prevent any general tightening of money. Alternatively, the government could eschew borrowing altogether and finance any deficit by the printing of new money. Such a possibility has been suggested by Abba P. Lerner, as will be seen in the second selection of readings in this volume. It has had little encouragement as a feasible course of action, in part because of the fear that this would remove any check on government spending and lead to the complete breakdown of fiscal responsibility. As noted above, however, this same argument is raised against any use of deficit spending, on the assumption that once governments are allowed to increase expenditures without a corresponding unpopular increase in taxes, there will be virtually no limit to their spending and increasing role in the economy. This view, which is identified with the position of classical economists, is not without its supporters today, and is strongly presented in the selection in these readings by the National Association of Manufacturers. Sidney S. Alexander, in an article included in this volume, emphasizes the view that much criticism of deficit spending is, in truth, due to the fear that its use for stabilization purposes increases the status as well as the role of government relative to that of business.

Combinations of expansionary fiscal policy other than the most obvious ones of raising expenditures and/or lowering taxes are possible, such as (1) increasing expenditures by an amount greater than a rise in taxes, (2) increasing taxes and expenditures by an equal amount, or even (3) having no change in the level of taxes and expenditures but changing their composition. One attraction of the latter two methods is the avoidance of a budget deficit.

By having an equal increase in taxes and expenditures the thought is that increased government expenditures will augment total spending by more than an equal rise in taxes will reduce it. This is due to the fact that spending is increased by the full amount of government outlay while not all of the income which is decreased by a tax rise would have been spent. Thus, in the first round of expenditures the tax increase reduces spending by less than an equivalent volume of government expenditures increases it. Assuming the same marginal propensity to consume for all changes in income, the tax rise and corresponding fall in income would lead to a decline in consumption equal to its increase in the second round of the multiplier process, following the initial addition to government expenditures and private incomes. Continuing this assumption that the marginal propensity to consume and therefore the multiplier are the same in both instances, all subsequent rounds of increase and decrease in spending would be equal. The final net effect would be an increase in income exactly equal to the original rise in taxes and expenditures, for a multiplier effect of one. This conclusion applies only to the very simplest model where other factors which may affect income are ignored, such as business savings, imports and exports. Using this approach to realize any given volume of expanded income, government expenditures would have to be increased by more than in the alternative method of engaging in deficit spending with its higher multiplier effect. Consequently, the price of avoiding a deficit would be to increase the government sector in the economy. This would seem to make sense only if a large increase in government spending were wanted for its own sake, because of a preference for collective versus private goods.

The conclusion that an equal increase in government spending and taxing is expansionary has not been accepted without dissent. One problem, which is similar to the one alluded to above in the case of borrowing to finance a budget deficit, is that the decrease in savings emanating from a tax rise leads to a decrease in available funds, a possible rise in interest rates, and a consequent decrease in investment. This could offset part or all of the expansionary effect from a rise in government spending being greater than the initial fall in consumer expenditures resulting from the tax cut. An answer to this criticism, again as suggested above, is that the cooperation of the monetary authorities can be enlisted to prevent any rise in interest rates. Among other criticisms is the proposition that the multiplier effect of decreased spending due to tax increases may be greater than for expenditure increases (although it can also be less) and that there are potential adverse incentive effects from increased taxes that may precipitate further drops in output and income. Most economists, however, would expect an equal expenditure-tax increase to have some expansionary effect.

In the second balanced budget approach, the argument is that a reshuffling of the tax and expenditure programs could stimulate a rise in income. In some circumstances, by changing taxes to have them fall more on savings and less on consumption, the net effect could be an increase in total spending. One method would be to make the tax system more progressive, if it is true that the marginal propensity to consume is greater for the lower than the higher income groups. Another method would be to shift from expenditures with relatively low multiplier effects to others which can be expected to be greater. Admittedly these kinds of changes in both taxes and expenditures are not easily accomplished in the short run and are probably of limited effectiveness.

One of the important points that this analysis demonstrates is that there are economic effects even within the framework of a balanced budget, that a balanced budget is not necessarily a neutral one. Further, it is not only the size of changes in taxes or expenditures that matters but also the types. As indicated, a reduction of income taxes for low income groups is likely to have a different effect on consumption, investment, and aggregate spending than an equal reduction for higher income groups, or for corporations; a decrease in excise tax rates on automobiles can have a different economic effect from an equal decrease in tax rates on alcohol. Similarly, in the case of expenditures, an increase in school construction would very likely lead to a different change in aggregate spending than, say, would result from an equal outlay in the hiring of more teachers.

Other questions which arise, when an expansionary fiscal program has been decided upon, are whether, from the points of view of maximizing welfare and political practicality, it is better to concentrate on tax cuts or expenditure increases. In general, those who believe we have more urgent needs in the public than the private sector would tend to favor the course of expenditure increases while those who believe the opposite will favor tax reduction. In the case of tax cuts those who would like to see a more equal distribution of income will prefer tax reduction primarily for the lower income groups, while others who believe that the tax system is already too progressive will favor more reductions for the higher income groups. In both of the above instances, either group might be willing to compromise its position if it is more concerned with the problem of stimulating the economy and it is felt that an approach at variance with the one it prefers has more chance of being enacted. Frequently, the controversy among economists and others on the issue of tax reduction versus expenditure increase and on the kind of change in either of these components reflects not so much a difference of opinion concerning economic effects as a difference of values. It is no accident that when discussing the best form of tax reduction to stimulate expansion, business spokesmen tend to emphasize relief for the higher income groups and corporations, while trade union spokesmen argue instead for a decrease in taxation on the middle and lower income groups. Surely, these views reflect, in large part, the interests and biases of the two groups.

As indicated at the outset, the tools of fiscal policy can also be used to stem an inflation caused by excessive spending. In this case the appropriate policies would be the reverse of those for bolstering demand and the simplest approach would be to raise taxes and/or lower expenditures. Again, many of the same issues and problems as those discussed above pertain. There are, however, some differences. One commonly held view is that, for political reasons, there may be more willingness to adopt fiscal policies designed to bolster a sluggish economy than to offset inflation. It is argued that it is politically easier both to lower taxes and increase spending than the reverse. Also, more political harm is incurred from conditions of economic slack with its attendant unemployment than from inflation with its usually accompanying prosperity for most. Accordingly, it is concluded, governments can be expected to be far quicker in adopting policies to combat unemployment than inflation so that the overall use of fiscal policy carries some bias toward the latter. It will be noted that Wilfred Lewis, Jr., in the last selection of these readings, questions this conclusion on the basis of his evaluation of the conduct of fiscal policy from 1948 to 1962.

A different kind of problem arises if there is an inflation caused, not by excessive demand, but rather by cost increases due to a rise in administered prices by large corporations with considerable market power and/or wages as a result of strong unionism and collective bargaining. This may occur even while there is considerable idleness in the economy. In this circumstance, adoption of a restrictive fiscal policy to halt the price rises may succeed, but only at the expense of increasing the extent of underutilization of resources in the economy. It may be that even without the influence of cost-push inflation there will be a tendency for the price level to rise in periods of full employment. In both these cases, fiscal policy is relatively helpless to achieve the goals of high-level income and employment on the one hand and price stability on the other. There may, indeed, be a basic conflict in the achievement of these twin goals and some choice has to be made as to what combination of resource utilization and general price increases, if any, is most desirable.

Along the same lines is the question of what leads to an economic decline or underutilization of resources. It may sometimes be due to a deficiency in aggregate demand, in which case expansionary fiscal policy is an appropriate response. It may at other times be caused by structural maladjustments due to cost-price distortions, rapid technological change, and other factors. In some of these cases, expansionary fiscal policy may yield only limited success because it does not solve the basic problem. It can perpetuate or even aggravate the fundamental malady and make the problem of sustaining prosperity in the long run more difficult. Fiscal policy may thus be a suitable tool for some but not all instances of inflation, on the one hand, and underutilization of resources on the other. In a number of cases it may serve little or no purpose, and different approaches are needed.

The problem of timing is another important issue in fiscal policy. Should the government, for example, anticipate an economic decline and adopt policies designed to head it off? This involves prediction. Is our forecasting ability good enough to warrant acting in this relatively bold manner? Or is it better to be more conservative and wait until an economic decline has begun before taking action? But here, too, lies peril. How can one be sure that an economic contraction, once begun, is going to continue? Perhaps it is destined to be a temporary abortive decline and one should wait six months or even a year before responding. At such a time, even if the decline had run its course and a recovery were about to begin, resources are likely to be sufficiently underutilized so that an extra stimulus by the government would be helpful. The trouble with this approach, however, is that, in addition to the fact that this permits resources to be excessively idle for a considerable period of time, too long a delay can allow cumulative forces to develop which become increasingly difficult to reverse except by the most massive use of fiscal policy.

To take the other side of the proposition, if the general price level has been rising due to the pressure of excess demand relative to resources should fiscal policy be restrictive to prevent a further rise? Perhaps the inflation is just about to end spontaneously. In that event such a policy may serve merely to usher in a recession. Again the problem hinges on our predictive skill.

If it is assumed that a particular prediction is reasonably accurate, there is the further problem concerning the inevitable delay required for legislative action. By the time a recommended program has been cleared through the legislature the original economic conditions may well have altered substantially in either direction, thus making the original plan unsuitable. A suggested solution to the dilemma thus posed is to grant the executive branch of government some discretionary authority and flexibility in the use of tax and expenditure policy such as the Federal Reserve Banks enjoy in the field of monetary policy. Congress, however, has to date shown no inclination to provide this.

It is apparent that conflicting goals cannot always be harmonized; the same is true for different tools. It was pointed out earlier in the introduction that it is important to have cooperation between monetary and fiscal policies. It has been our experience, however, that because of different objectives, this is not always routinely possible. For example, in the year 1963, the predominant view was to have an expansionary fiscal program, and this was finally implemented in the tax reduction bill which was passed early in 1964. At the same time, the monetary authorities were caught between a desire to lower interest rates to stimulate the private economy and raise them to help redress an unfavorable balance of payments position. Higher interest rates help solve the latter problem by encouraging foreigners to invest in the United States and keeping Americans from investing as much abroad. At the same time, however, these same higher interest rates probably have some adverse effect on domestic investment and so work at cross purposes to expansionist policies. In another instance, that of the immediate post-World War II period, there was another conflict between fiscal and monetary policy. Especially in the years 1946–1948 and again in 1950–1951 the prevailing view was that fiscal policy should follow a contractionary course to help stem inflation and to a certain extent this was done. In harmony with this approach the monetary authorities, too, should have adopted a restrictive policy. They were precluded from doing this due to the pursuit of another goal, that of supporting the government bond market. This led to the purchase of government securities by the Federal Reserve Banks in order to maintain bond prices and the result was an increase in the reserves of the banking system, the maintenance of low interest rates, and a generally easy expansionary monetary policy. Such conflict of policies need not lead to frustration and failure. If, as in 1963–1964 or at any other time, it is decided that monetary policy cannot be expansionist due to balance of payments problems, this calls for more stimulus from fiscal policy than would otherwise be necessary. The conflict does, however, increase the burden on fiscal policy and is presented here as a specific illustration of a possible obstacle to its success.

PART ONE

THE CASE FOR A BALANCED BUDGET: THE VIEW OF CLASSICAL ECONOMISTS

JESSE BURKHEAD

The Balanced Budget*

In this article Burkhead presents and evaluates the views of leading classical and neoclassical economists on the issues of budget balancing and the public debt. Of the authors included in his survey, one, Thomas Malthus, sees some merit in the public debt as a means of raising the level of consumption through the spending of interest receipts by the debt owners. This implies the dubious assumption that the debt holders have a higher marginal propensity to consume than those who are taxed to finance the interest payments. Although the other authors emphasize different points, they unite in their opposition to borrowing and government debt. A primary reason for their objection to deficits is the contention that, by removing the need to levy painful taxes, the government can be expected to indulge in an extravagant increase in its expenditures. This would diminish private spending on productive capital goods due to the diversion of savings to the purchase of government securities and thus reduce economic

---

   * Abridged and reprinted by permission of the publishers from *The Quarterly Journal of Economics* (May 1954). Cambridge, Mass.: Harvard University Press. Copyright, 1954, by the President and Fellows of Harvard College.

progress and wealth. It is even argued that allowance of budget deficits could lead governments to engage in unnecessary wars because of the ease of financing them. In addition to generating waste, it is contended that the increased volume of public expenditures, which is assumed to result from borrowing, will very likely cause currency depreciation due to the generation of excessive demand, and also due to the government's interest in promoting inflation as a means of reducing the burden of the resulting debt. With the exception of Malthus, the classical economists as a group did not see the need for any program, fiscal or otherwise, for stimulating the economy. Full employment was assumed and government spending could be increased only at the expense of a decline in the private use of resources. Based on the two assumptions of full employment and the inherently irresponsible nature of government, strong opposition to public borrowing and deficit spending is the inevitable conclusion.

It is commonly held that the classicists assumed that the economic role of the state must necessarily be limited and they then adduced certain rationalizations regarding the nature of governmental fiscal operations to support this assumption. It seems more likely that such economists as Adam Smith looked first at the objective requirements of the economic order and then proceeded to theorize about the proper role of the state therein.[1]

Adam Smith's views on balanced budgets were conditioned very largely by his views on national debt.[2] And his views on the latter are a clear and direct product of his antimercantilism. It is difficult to dissociate Smith, the antimercantile-polemicist, from Smith the economist. His often quoted passages defining, in restrictive terms, the proper and legitimate functions of the state should probably be viewed not so much as an evidence of his pro-laissez-faire position as an evidence of his antimercantilism. Smith was an antimercantilist because he saw that the state apparatus as it then existed was an

[1] See Harvey S. Perloff, "Budgetary Symbolism and Fiscal Planning," *Public Policy*, II, Graduate School of Public Administration, Harvard University, pp. 40–44.

[2] For a discussion of pre-Smithian practices and views on these matters see C. F. Bastable, *Public Finance* (London: Macmillan and Co., Ltd., 1922), pp. 611–57; Gustav Cohn, *The Science of Finance*, trans. T. B. Veblen (Chicago: University of Chicago Press, 1895), pp. 691–703.

inefficient organization from the standpoint of wealth and income creation. It was the bulwark of a pattern of special trading privileges, grants of monopoly and tariffs. More importantly, the state was wasteful; it took funds from merchants and industrialists and spent these funds in riotous living. This deprived industry and commerce of capital which was badly needed for the furtherance of production and trade by diverting the national product toward consumer goods and away from capital goods.

This was the major reason for Smith's opposition to unbalanced budgets: governments would borrow from industry and commerce and thus deprive a capital-poor society of revenue which could be productively reinvested.[3] From this major ground for opposition to public borrowing stemmed other arguments. Once the sovereign started to borrow, his political power was increased, because he was no longer dependent on tax exactions from his subjects. Therefore, borrowing encouraged the sovereign to wage needless wars. On the other hand, if taxes were raised to meet current costs, "Wars would in general be more speedily concluded, and less wantonly undertaken."[4] In short, the ability to engage in loan finance makes for irresponsibility in the sovereign.

England's experience with national debt after the beginning of the eighteenth century adequately justified Smith's concern. In the years from 1713 to 1739 the South Sea Bubble and the war with Spain had added to the national debt. The war of 1739 – 48 raised England's debt from £47,000,000 to £78,000,000. At the end of the Seven Years' War in 1763, the debt stood at about £136,000,000. Furthermore, the intervening peacetime years did not bring important debt reductions.[5]

For Smith these increases in debt were most serious when they were *created;* the burden of an *existing* debt, although important, was much less significant. The most important loss came when industry and trade lent their funds to the state. Contemporaries of Smith had pointed out that an internally-held debt occasioned no loss through the annual interest transfer from taxpayers to bondholders. Smith replied that, "This apology is founded altogether in the sophistry of the mercantile system, . . ."[6] In confounding the sophistry Smith

[3] Adam Smith, *The Wealth of Nations,* Cannan edition (London: Methuen & Co., Ltd., 1930), II, 409–11.

[4] *Ibid.,* p. 411.

[5] Bastable, *op. cit.,* pp. 630–32.

[6] Smith, *op. cit.,* p. 412.

contended that the public creditor was not a good manager. Unlike the private creditor, he ". . . has no interest . . . in the good management of any particular portion of capital stock."[7] Further, the annual tax burdens occasioned by the interest payment may drive capital from the country. "The industry of the country will necessarily fall with the removal of the capital which supported it, and the ruin of trade and manufactures will necessarily follow the declension of agriculture."[8]

And, finally, there is a long-run danger in the debt. Once "accumulated to a certain degree" it leads inevitably to national bankruptcy. Since the days of Rome, sovereigns had resorted to all manner of juggling and trickery to "liberate the revenue." Bankruptcy had been disguised by "pretended payments" in debased currency; sovereigns adulterated the coin.[9]

Jean-Baptiste Say, conditioned no doubt by a French debt experience which was even more irresponsible than the English, was as vehement as Smith in opposition to debts and deficits. He was very much impressed with the wastefulness of government outlay, and cited example after example to the point.[10] The sovereign is engaged in pomp and circumstance, the preservation of etiquette and custom is a very expensive affair. The wealth which passes from the hands of the taxpayer to the taxgatherer is consumed and destroyed.

Say based these views on the argument that public consumption is not, in principle, different from the consumption of individuals or families. In either case there is a destruction of values and a loss of wealth.[11] The limitation of public consumption, like the limitation of private consumption, is necessary to provide capital for industry and trade. Public borrowing is not only unproductive because the capital is consumed and lost, but, in addition, the nation is burdened by the annual interest payment. It cannot be argued that the annual circulation of interest payments is a net addition to capital. "The

[7] *Ibid.*, p. 413.

[8] *Loc. cit.*

[9] *Ibid.*, pp. 415–18.

[10] "It would be curious to calculate the time wasted in the toilet, or to estimate, if possible, the many dearly-paid hours lost, in the course of the last century, on the road between Paris and Versailles." J. B. Say, *A Treatise on Political Economy*, translated from the 4th edition by C. R. Prinsep (Philadelphia: Lippincott, Grambo & Co., 1853), p. 428.

[11] *Ibid.*, p. 412.

tax-payer would have spent what is now spent by the public creditor; that is all."[12]

A national debt of moderate amount which had been judiciously expanded in useful public works might be attended by the advantage of providing an investment outlet for the minute forms of capital which might otherwise be squandered by individuals.

This is perhaps the sole benefit of a national debt; and even this is attended with some danger, inasmuch as it enables a government to squander the national savings. For, unless the principal be spent upon objects of permanent public benefit, as on roads, canals or the like, it were better for the public, that the capital should remain inactive, or concealed; since, if the public lost the use of it, at least it would not have to pay the interest.[13]

It is irresponsible government which is to be feared. When the government credit is strong, Say said (apparently quoting with approval from contemporary political scientists):

they are too apt to intermeddle in every political arrangement, and to conceive gigantic projects, that lead sometimes to disgrace, sometimes to glory, but always to a state of financial exhaustion; to make war themselves, and stir up others to do the like; to subsidize every mercenary agent, and deal in the blood and the consciences of mankind; making capital, which should be the fruit of industry and virtue, the prize of ambition, pride, and wickedness.[14]

It is not surprising that David Ricardo, writing at the end of the Napoleonic Wars, should have generally shared the antipathy of his classical predecessors to national debt. By 1816 England's debt stood at about £500,000,000, approximately double what it had been at the turn of the century.[15] It was appropriate, in these circumstances, for Ricardo to refer to the debt as ". . . one of the most terrible scourges which was ever invented to afflict a nation. . ."[16] However, by this time the industrialization of England was much further advanced than it had been in 1776. Irresponsible sovereigns, in

[12] *Ibid.,* p. 480.

[13] *Ibid.,* p. 481.

[14] *Ibid.,* p. 483.

[15] Bastable, *op. cit.,* pp. 634–35.

[16] David Ricardo, "Funding System," *The Works and Correspondence of David Ricardo,* Vol. IV, ed. Piero Sraffa and M. H. Dobb (Cambridge, England, 1951), p. 197.

league with merchant-princes, were no longer the threat to economic progress that they had been in Smith's time. The national debt was a significant problem, but in his *Principles*, Ricardo did not devote the attention to this subject that Smith had. When he did discuss it, Ricardo made important modifications in the arguments of Smith and Say.[17]

Ricardo pointed out that the important burden of the national debt was not in the annual interest transfer, but in the loss of original capital:

When, for the expenses of a year's war, twenty millions are raised by means of a loan, it is the twenty millions which are withdrawn from the productive capital of the nation. The million per annum which is raised by taxes to pay the interest of this loan, is merely transferred from those who pay it to those who receive it, from the contributor to the tax, to the national creditor. The real expense is the twenty millions, and not the interest which must be paid for it.[18]

The effects of the annual interest transfer, Ricardo argued, would depend on what A and B, taxpayer and creditor, did with the revenue. Either A or B might squander the revenue; either might employ it productively. The annual transfer was in no sense lost to the economy.

Once a nation has incurred a debt, no great *economic* advantage accrues from retiring it. The presence of the debt does not affect the nation's ability to pay taxes. There is the same taxable capital with or without the debt:

It is not, then, by the payment of the interest on the national debt, that a country is distressed, nor is it by the exoneration from payment that it can be relieved. It is only by saving from income, and retrenching in expenditure, that the national capital can be increased; and neither the income would be increased, nor the expenditure diminished by the annihilation of the national debt.[19]

Neither does the presence of the debt place the nation at any particular disadvantage with respect to foreign countries. Taxes will be higher, it is true, and the price of labor will be increased, but the real capital of the nation is unchanged; the only problem is a transfer problem.

[17] David Ricardo, *Principles of Political Economy and Taxation, The Works and Correspondence of David Ricardo*, Vol. I, pp. 243–49.

[18] *Ibid.*, p. 244.

[19] *Ibid.*, p. 246.

Why, then, should the national debt be retired? Why does it justify the appellation of "scourge"? Here Ricardo shifts ground and abandons aggregative analysis to contend that, even though there is no loss of capital in the aggregate, the particular taxes which may be levied to pay the interest will encourage every individual contributor to "withdraw his shoulder from the burthen," and,

> . . . the temptation to remove himself and his capital to another country, where he will be exempted from such burthens, becomes at last irresistible, and overcomes the natural reluctance which every man feels to quit the place of his birth, and the scene of his early associations. . . . That which is wise in an individual, is wise also in a nation.[20]

Ricardo's most important writing on the national debt was the essay on the funding system, contributed to the *Encyclopaedia Britannica.* His contemporary, Dr. Robert Hamilton, had authored *An Inquiry Concerning the Rise and Progress, the Redemption, and Present State of the National Debt of Great Britain,* which included a critical attack on the debt retirement schemes which had been in force since 1716. The sinking fund schemes had not proved efficacious in eliminating the debt; ministers always abused the arrangements. Ricardo was apparently in essential agreement with Hamilton in his criticism of these schemes and in this essay he elaborated Hamilton's arguments and discussed at some length the distinctions between annual revenue, paid as interest on the debt, or as contribution to the sinking fund, and the capital of taxpayers which was available for productive investment.[21] Although in his *Principles,* Ricardo had pointed out the limitations in the arguments of those who advocated retirement of the debt, in the *Britannica* article he simply assumed that debt retirement was desirable.

Ricardo proposed that in future (war) emergencies the government adopt a pay-as-you-go financial plan. Thus, "When the pressure of war is felt at once, without mitigation, we shall be less disposed wantonly to engage in an expensive contest, and if engaged in it, we shall be sooner disposed to get out of it, unless it be a contest for some great national interest."[22] A pay-as-you-go plan might encourage a higher level of current saving, in order to meet the temporarily heavier taxes. At the termination of hostilities there would be no continued interest (and taxation) burden. Further, to

---

[20] *Ibid.,* pp. 247–48.
[21] "Funding System," *op. cit.,* pp. 149–200.
[22] *Ibid.,* p. 186.

extinguish the outstanding debt, Ricardo proposed a once-over special levy of two or three years' duration on property. Thus, "by one great effort" we should get rid of this "terrible scourge."[23]

The dissenter, whose views on public debt ought to be examined before continuing the main stream of classical development, is Thomas Robert Malthus. The national debt is not the evil which it is generally supposed to be, said Malthus. Those who live on the interest from the national debt, like statesmen, soldiers and sailors, ". . .contribute powerfully to distribution and demand. . . . they ensure that effective consumption which is necessary to give the proper stimulus to production. . . ."[24] Therefore, the debt, once created, is not a great evil:

It is, I know, generally thought that all would be well, if we could but be relieved from the very heavy burden of our debt. And yet I feel perfectly convinced that, if a sponge could be applied to it tomorrow, and we could put out of our consideration the poverty and misery of the public creditors, by supposing them to be supported comfortably in some other country, the rest of the society, as a nation, instead of being enriched, would be impoverished. It is the greatest mistake to suppose that the landlords and capitalists would either at once, or in a short time, be prepared for so great an additional consumption as such a change would require;. . . and I feel very little doubt that, in five years from the date of such an event, not only would the exchangeable value of the whole produce, estimated in domestic and foreign labour, be decidedly diminished, but a smaller absolute quantity of corn would be grown, and fewer manufactured and foreign commodities would be brought to market than before.[25]

Since the greatest powers of production are comparatively use-less without effective consumption, Malthus argued, ". . . it would be the height of rashness to determine, under all circumstances, that the sudden diminution of the national debt and the removal of taxa-tion must necessarily tend to increase the national wealth, and pro-vide employment for the labouring classes."[26] But having made his case as forcibly as possible, Malthus almost immediately modified his position to bring it closer to that of his classical colleagues. There are, after all, evils in the debt. The taxation which is required to

---

[23] *Ibid.,* p. 197.

[24] Thomas R. Malthus, *Principles of Political Economy* (2d ed.; London: William Pickering, 1836), p. 409.

[25] Notes on Malthus's *Principles of Political Economy, The Works and Correspondence of David Ricardo,* Vol. II, pp. 434–35. To this Ricardo replied, "I should think that Mr. Malthus must be the only man in England who would expect such effects from such a cause." (*Ibid.*)

[26] Malthus, *op. cit.,* p. 411.

meet the interest payments may be harmful; people think the debt should be paid off, so the interest on it is always to some degree "insecure"; the presence of the debt aggravates the evils arising from changes in the value of money.[27] These disadvantages must be weighed carefully against the advantage of maintaining a body of "unproductive consumers" who encourage wealth by maintaining a balance between production and consumption. The need for the unproductive consumers, in turn, varies with time and place, and the skill and tastes of a people.

In 1848 John Stuart Mill could appropriately suggest some further modifications in the body of classical thinking on national debt and deficits. Apparently, by this time industry's need for capital was not as pressing as it had been earlier. In some circumstances, Mill said, government loans are not charged with pernicious consequences.

. . . first, when what is borrowed is foreign capital, the overflowings of the general accumulation of the world; or, secondly, when it is capital which either would not have been saved at all, unless this mode of investment had been open to it, or, after being saved, would have been wasted in unproductive enterprises, or sent to seek employment in foreign countries.[28]

Further, Mill suggested an "index" for determining whether there are pernicious consequences stemming from government loans. If the loan raises the rate of interest it could be concluded that capital is taken which could have been productively employed, and ". . . those loans are chargeable with all the evils which have been described."[29] But if interest rates are unchanged, the pernicious consequences are not evident.

Mill continued to stress that government borrowing is harmful if it destroys capital which could otherwise be used for productive employment.[30] However, he finds it somewhat paradoxical that in these years of capital destruction — mainly war years — there is apparent prosperity. He concluded that this occurs because loan finance is an effective subtraction from the portion employed in paying laborers, and the laborers suffer accordingly. But if production is the same, the country is no poorer. "The breach made in the

[27] *Ibid.*, pp. 411–12.

[28] John Stuart Mill, *Principles of Political Economy*, Ashley edition (London: Longmans, Green and Co., 1929), p. 874.

[29] *Ibid.*, p. 874. Mill obviously assumed that there is a "free" market in funds and that supply is relatively inelastic.

[30] *Ibid.*, pp. 76–78.

capital of the country is thus instantly repaired, but repaired by the privations and often the real misery of the labouring class."[31]

Regardless of whether a country has wisely or unwisely incurred a national debt, it is expedient to pay it off as rapidly as possible.[32] Mill discussed the two methods available — immediate payment by a general contribution and gradual payment with surplus revenue, and concluded that the former was preferable but that the latter was more practicable.

After J. S. Mill, the major classical economists devoted less and less attention to problems of the national debt. This is evidently a direct reflection of the fact that from this time until 1914 the outstanding British debt remained almost constant. The increase at the time of the Boer War was wiped out by debt reduction in the immediately subsequent years. At the same time, the level of national income increased tremendously; Britain grew out of her debt.[33] The writings of the classicists of this period reflected the lesser significance of the debt. Cairnes, in 1874, has no organized discussion of national debt or government financial problems. Sidgwick, writing in 1883, briefly discusses the effects of government borrowing, but adds little to the views of J. S. Mill.[34]

[31] *Ibid.*, p. 76.

[32] It seems to be characteristic of Ricardo, Malthus and Mill that after partially destroying the "scourge concept" of the national debt they embrace it in their policy conclusions. It is almost as if they are arguing, "The debt is not so bad as is supposed, but nevertheless we ought to pay it off."

[33] The ratio of debt service to national income was about the same in 1923 as it had been in 1818. (See *Report of the Committee on National Debt and Taxation,* Cmd. 2800, pp. 235–36.)

[34] Sidgwick incorporates in his discussion the distinction between productive and unproductive government debt, a distinction observed but not fully developed by his predecessors and also suggests that borrowing tends to increase inequality in the distribution of national wealth. (Henry Sidgwick, *The Principles of Political Economy* (3d ed.; London: Macmillan and Co., 1901), pp. 549–53.)

The main body of American writing on governmental financial policy did not differ in general outlook from that of the British classicists in the last half of the nineteenth century. Henry C. Adams, for example, was as strong, but no stronger in his condemnation of public debts and deficit financing than his British contemporaries. (Henry C. Adams, *Public Debts,* p. 78.) The prevalence of these views in the United States indicates not only the strength of the classical outlook but also the triumph of Gallatin's position over Hamilton's. The latter had contended forcibly that any evils inherent in the debt were more than offset by the advantages derived from a high level of federal expenditures and from the resulting stability of private credit. Gallatin, however, had apparently been more influenced by *The Wealth of Nations* and was in general

The culmination of the classical tradition — Marshall's *Principles* — devotes no attention whatever to the subject. And, significantly enough, the passing references to national debt in Marshall's *Money, Credit and Commerce* exhibit almost no concern for the problem, even though this book appeared immediately after World War I. Marshall's attitude toward the possibly wasteful spending practices of the sovereign is strikingly different from Smith's:

The work of credit in the modern age differs from that of earlier times. . . . Formerly a great part of it was given by professional money-lenders to spendthrift heirs; now it is chiefly given by people who are living within their incomes to States which do not spend recklessly; and to strong businesses. . . . Monarchs used to be large borrowers: chiefly for the purposes of war; largely to support extravagance on the part of themselves and their favorites; and occasionally for financing expenditure on good roads, and other requisites of national well-being. . . .[35]

At about the turn of the century public finance dropped out of the main stream of classical economics and developed as a partially independent "science of finance." The views of Bastable are representative of this approach.[36]

It seems likely that Bastable, writing the first edition of *Public Finance* in 1892, was influenced by the German and French writings and experience in government finance, and possibly by the financial practices of private industry.[37] Whatever the reason, Bastable now

---

agreement with Jefferson's pungent phrase that the national debt was "swindling futurity on a large scale." (For a summary of this controversy see Paul Studenski and Herman E. Kroos, *Financial History of the United States,* pp. 69–71; also, George Rogers Taylor (ed.), *Hamilton and the National Debt;* Henry Adams (ed.), *The Writings of Albert Gallatin,* III, pp. 143–52.)

35 Alfred Marshall, *Money, Credit, and Commerce,* pp. 69–70.

36 The style of writing on this subject altered drastically from the time of Smith and Say to the time of Bastable. For the former, the history of governmental financial practice was cited for purposes of drawing a moral, or citing a horrible example of malpractice. With Bastable, history is history — this happened, and that was said. The issues are no longer burning. One can afford to be dispassionate.

37 A wholly different view of the role and function of public credit was developed by the German economists in the last half of the nineteenth century. This approach stressed the "productive" character of much public expenditure and the role that public credit had played in the development of private credit instruments. It further argued that governments could appropriately borrow for permanent improvements that would benefit future generations. For an excellent discussion of this literature, and German national and state financial policy which accompanied it, see Gustav Cohn, *op. cit.,* pp. 718–26.

This approach seems to have had very little impact on the literature or prac-

presses the ". . .fundamental difference between two classes of debt, the one contracted for non-economic ends, the other for purposes of reproductive employment."[38] This distinction should not be stretched, however, to embrace nonrevenue producing assets.[39] "National culture, education, the promotion of social progress are all most desirable; but their promotion is not so urgently required as to need the use of borrowing by the public powers."[40] It is appropriate to finance the purchase of the Prussian railways or the English telegraphs by borrowing, but not the construction of school buildings. The latter may be generally and indirectly productive, but the results of such expenditure are ". . .hard to trace or measure, and any statement respecting them must rest in a great degree on conjecture."[41]

Unless there is an equivalent revenue obtained from the application of the proceeds of borrowing, Bastable argued, there will inevitably be a curtailment of the future power of spending. Heavy borrowing cripples the ordinary revenue and compels retrenchment in the future. However, there are conditions under which loan finance is to be preferred to heavy taxation. Nonrecurrent and large expenditures may be financed by loans with less disturbance than if heavy taxation were used. Where the expenditure extends over a period of years, there may be limits to the productiveness of specific taxes and of the tax system as a whole, so that borrowing is necessary. And, in some circumstances, it may not be politically expedient to press heavily on the taxpayers.[42] In developing an adequate financial policy for a government it is of greatest importance to have a budget system, and a strong minister of finance who will undertake "prudent reduction of outlay" and "skilful adjustment of resources."[43] ". . . the

tice of fiscal policy in Great Britain and the United States, unless it can be contended that the distinction between productive and unproductive debt came from this source. However, in the Keynesian attack on classical fiscal principles, some inspiration was apparently derived from the most prominent of the German writers of the nineteenth century. See Walter F. Stettner, "Carl Ditzel, Public Expenditures, and the Public Debt," in Lloyd A. Metzler (ed.), *Income, Employment and Public Policy*, pp. 276–99.

[38] Bastable, *op. cit.*, p. 627.

[39] *Ibid.*, p. 670.

[40] *Loc. cit.*

[41] *Ibid.*, p. 671.

[42] *Ibid.*, pp. 678–79.

[43] *Ibid.*, pp. 734–36.

creation of the budget is therefore a work of administrative art, in which the use of proper methods will very materially improve the financial position, and contribute to the public advantage."[44]

A final and important addition to this body of doctrine developed from the application of the principles of marginalism to public finance. Marginalism in public finance seems to have been first elaborated as a conceptual framework for analyzing the distribution of tax burdens, then applied to the distribution of government expenditures, and finally utilized to bring together the revenue and expenditure activities of government.[45] Dalton's is one of the first complete elaborations of this approach:

Public expenditure in every direction should be carried just so far, that the advantage to the community of a further small increase in any direction is just counterbalanced by the disadvantage of a corresponding small increase in taxation or in receipts from any other source of public income. This gives the ideal total both of public expenditure and of public income.[46]

It may be assumed that public income from borrowing involves no disutilities to the lender. Therefore, utilities and disutilities are balanced when the budget is balanced.[47]

From this summary account of the classical approach to budget balancing and national debt it is evident that attitudes and analyses changed substantially from the time of Smith to the time of Bastable and Dalton. Perhaps the greatest change is that the degree of antipathy to debts and deficits was modified sharply downward.

In spite of the changes it is possible to summarize the classical doctrine in a set of propositions, intermingled though the propositions are. In some cases these are clearly set forth in the writings of the classicists. In other cases they must be inferred. Parts of the doctrine were accepted by some but rejected by other writers. These

[44] *Ibid.*, p. 736.

[45] Emil Sax is credited with being the first to apply marginalism to public finance. For an excellent discussion of the development of this approach see Mabel L. Walker, *Municipal Expenditures*, pp. 28–51.

[46] Hugh Dalton, *Principles of Public Finance*, pp. 18–19.

[47] Smithies has pointed out that the application of marginalism to the division of resources between public and private use does not require a balanced budget where there is a defined fiscal policy goal of raising the money level of national income and where tax reduction is one of the means available for reaching this goal. However, this possibility was not considered by the marginalists; for them, budget balancing was the end product of the application of their principles. (See Arthur Smithies, "Federal Budgeting and Fiscal Policy," *A Survey of Contemporary Economics*, I, 192–95.)

propositions on debts and deficits, together with an assessment of their current validity, are as follows:

1. Government loan finance withdraws funds from productive private employment.

Where this point is interpreted to mean that an economy has an aggregate funds shortage it is a generalization which has no applicability whatsoever in an advanced industrial economy possessed of a fractional reserve banking system and central banking techniques. Government bonds sold to commercial banks and to the central bank do not absorb funds which would otherwise be invested in the private sector. Indeed, J. S. Mill, as noted, did not attempt to support this generalization so long ago as 1848. Where the argument is advanced, as it was by Say, to mean that funds should be expended on capital goods by industry rather than on consumer goods by the state, what is really implied is that government expenditures do not add to productive capacity and that there are unfulfilled investment opportunities in industry and trade. This makes the point much more complex and eliminates any general validity which it may possess.

2. Deficits are less painful than current taxes. Unbalanced budgets therefore expand governmental activity and invite irresponsible governmental action.

There is no doubt that deficits are relatively painless, as compared with increased taxes, but it is much less certain that deficit spending necessarily leads to irresponsibility, unless it has been defined in advance as equivalent to irresponsibility. In a modern budgetary system it would be most difficult to demonstrate that the legislature scrutinizes less closely the outlays financed by loans than the outlays financed by taxes, or that wartime deficits or deficits incurred to combat a depression represent a fiscal policy which is more irresponsible than peacetime surpluses.

The point at issue here is the general one of securing a responsible and democratic government. The emergence of such government over the last several hundred years is not at all equivalent to the avoidance of governmental deficits. Modern budgetary systems have been most important in the development of responsible government but their contribution is not to be judged solely in terms of the elimination of deficits.

There is another point which remains in this argument, the point which Adam Smith was most concerned about. Deficit finance expands the relative power of government, vis-à-vis the taxpayers. Where governments can control resources without immediately diverting them from private incomes, there is, beyond doubt, an augmentation in the political and economic power of the sovereign. If the sovereign is irresponsible, he will resort to loan finance under conditions where it is not justified; loan finance, in turn, will increase his power. Strict adherence to the limitations of a balanced budget will operate to restrict the growth of the public sector.

3. Government borrowing makes future financing more difficult by increasing the proportion of the budget which must go for fixed charges and by increasing the amount of taxes which must be paid to finance the transfer of interest on the debt.

This proposition is applicable and important to the extent that governmental revenues are restricted by constitutional, statutory or economic factors. Therefore, it is more applicable to state and local governments than to a national government. Moreover, for a strong national government, the increase in fixed charges and accompanying taxes may be offset by lowered interest rates, unless there are institutional barriers which require orthodox financial practices. Additions to government debt need not bring higher tax rates, even with the level of national income unchanged, if interest rates are continuously brought down by central monetary authority.

Where interest payments do increase, together with taxes, to support these payments, the possibly deleterious consequences depend, as Ricardo pointed out, on the pattern of taxpaying and the pattern of bondholding. A domestically-held debt is burdensome in so far as the transfer is burdensome. Economic burdens will obtain only where the additional taxes levied to finance the interest payments discourage economic activity more than the receipts of interest encourage it.[48]

4. Loan finance is costly; public outlays financed in this way must be paid for twice — once in meeting interest charges and once in amortizing the debt.

Viewed as a matter of arithmetic, this proposition cannot be

[48] This subject received much attention in the years immediately after World War II when public and professional concern over the national debt was at its height. In one careful analysis of the problem it was concluded that interest on the federal debt, and the corresponding pattern of tax payments to support that interest, operated moderately in the direction of reducing concentration in the distribution of total income, a consequence which is desirable if the economy is tending toward underconsumption. See Henry C. Wallich, "The Changing Significance of the Interest Rate," *American Economic Review*, Dec. 1946, pp. 770–75. Also, Jacob Cohen, "Distributional Effects of the Federal Debt," *Journal of Finance*, Sept. 1951, pp. 267–75; Jesse V. Burkhead, "Full Employment and Interest-Free Borrowing," *Southern Economic Journal*, July 1947, pp. 1–13.

doubted. Where debts are amortized, the finance of capital outlay by means of borrowing entails an increasing volume of annual charges which soon mount to the point where less outlay is possible than if all financing had been undertaken out of current revenue.[49] However, as in the case of budgetary inflexibility, the importance of "costliness" must be judged in relation to the nature of the governmental receipts and expenditures.

The "costliness" of governmental borrowing, again, is most serious for governmental units with limited tax and credit resources. It is not hard to convince city officials that a pay-as-you-go plan for municipal improvements is to be preferred to loan finance; the latter is too expensive. The interest payments may be a serious drain on a city's financial resources, and the interest payments are likely to be made "abroad," that is, to bondholders outside the city's jurisdiction.

But "costliness" in these terms does not apply to the federal government of the United States. Here the interest payments are not made "abroad"; instead, they are transfer payments within the economy.

Of these propositions the first and fourth appear to possess little validity. The second — that deficits expand the scope of governmental power — is significant, particularly where government officials and legislators are irresponsible and require the fiscal discipline of rigid rule-making. The third — that debt finance raises the level of future tax payments — is important in those cases where governments choose to make it so, that is, where policy decisions are limited by fiscal orthodoxy. . . .

5. Unbalanced budgets contribute to currency deterioration.

There is no doubt that, from the time of Adam Smith to the present day, unbalanced budgets have evoked great concern on this ground. History, even recent history, is replete with cases of corrupt or inefficient governments which went to their ruin in a shower of paper currency.

Unbalanced budgets could conceivably lead to inflation in one of two ways. Either the deficit itself could be inflationary, as governments made net contributions to levels of demand, or the accumulated deficits, by their additions to money supply, could contribute to inflationary pressure. These influences are not always separated in popular discussion.[50]

---

[49] For a demonstration of this point, see James A. Maxwell, "The Capital Budget," this *Journal*, May 1943, pp. 454–56.

[50] For Adam Smith it was the debt itself which produced the currency

It is almost a truism that governmental deficits add to levels of effective demand and that unless the supply of resources is elastic at current price levels, prices will rise. However, from this relationship it should not be concluded that an increase in the federal deficit will inevitably lead to an increase in prices. Examination of the behavior of the wholesale price index and federal deficits since 1930 shows that it has not worked out this way. In only eight of the twenty-three fiscal years from July 1, 1930 to June 30, 1953 was there a positive association between an increase in the federal deficit and an increase in the price level. In fifteen of these years changes in the deficit and changes in wholesale prices moved in opposite directions. In some recent years the inverse association has been striking. In fiscal 1951 the budget moved from a deficit of $3.1 billion to a surplus of $3.5 billion, that is a *decrease* in the deficit of $6.6 billion. In the same fiscal years there was an *increase* in the wholesale price level by 15 per cent. In fiscal 1953 the budget deficit increased from $4.0 billion to $9.3 billion, but the level of wholesale prices dropped slightly.

It is evident that in any one year currency stability cannot be assured by balancing the budget.[51] It can be assured only by "balancing" the combined operation of the government and the private sectors. If the outlook is inflation, then, clearly, a balanced or overbalanced budget is not out of order. But there can be no assurance that the surplus will not be offset by activities in the private sector.

It is very frequently contended that accumulated deficits (debt) are an inflationary force. The additions to money supply occasioned by the debt may add to bank reserves, which, in the absence of countervailing action, may encourage banks to extend loans to business firms and households. Debt holdings by persons, by adding to the stock of liquid assets, may conceivably lead to a higher consumption ratio out of current income. Business firms may liquidate their

deterioration, as sovereigns attempted to reduce its crushing burden by clipping coins and printing paper money. This view, surely, was the product of an age of irresponsible sovereigns, and of a time when at least in part, the debts of the state were the personal debts of the crown, to be retired in depreciated currency when the crown could temporarily gain an advantage over the merchant-bondholders with whom it was engaged in a more or less continual struggle. Smith did not argue that there was a causal relation between current deficits and currency depreciation.

[51] It should also be noted that balancing the federal budget balances only a set of accounts, which are not the whole of federal financial operations. Trust accounts are excluded from the budget and their surpluses or deficits are excluded from the definition of budget surplus or deficit.

debt holdings to bid up the price of inventory or producers' durables. Debt holdings by the public are thus an inflationary potential, which, if not offset by other controls, may be a destabilizing influence. But again, the point to be stressed is that accumulated deficits and the concomitant increased liquidity do not, in themselves, generate an inflationary movement. They may feed it but they do not start it. Liquidity is significant only in relation to its distribution among those who are motivated to make their demands effective. It is not significant in the aggregate. Liquid asset holdings did not prevent the 1949 recession.

6. A balanced budget provides an easily-understood rule to guide the transfer of resources from the private to the public sector.

Here the advocates of budget balancing appear to be on firm ground. Whether or not this proposition is grounded in the economics of marginal utilities and disutilities, there is no doubt that budget balancing, particularly annual budget balancing, has a definite and precise character which is lacking in any other available guide to fiscal policy.[52] The concept of "balancing over the business cycle," for example, always generates uncertainty as to the precise point in the cycle where one finds oneself. Moreover, budget balancing is a practicable guide for policy-making officials, who can roughly gauge the amount of taxation which the community can "stand" and then trim expenditures to fit the revenue.

Unfortunately, however, this guideline is valueless when there are unemployed resources which may be put to work producing goods and services. The employment of such resources is virtually costless to the economy as a whole. In the vocabulary of the marginalists, there are only utilities — no disutilities.

---

[52] For the limitations which attach to a strict application of marginalism in this area see A. C. Pigou, *A Study in Public Finance* (3d rev. ed., London: Macmillan & Co. Ltd., 1951), pp. 31–34.

PART TWO

THE CASE FOR FEDERAL DEFICITS
TO COMBAT UNEMPLOYMENT

ABBA P. LERNER

Functional Finance and
the Federal Debt*

Lerner presents the case for compensatory fiscal policy in almost dramatically simple terms. In direct contrast to the predominant pre-1930's view, summarized in the preceding selection, that taxes are needed to balance a given level of expenditures, he argues that their sole function should be to limit spending in order to prevent inflation. The same basic principle applies to borrowing which should be used as a means, say, of absorbing savings or directing liquid assets into particular channels. If there were not these or other economic reasons for borrowing, there is nothing wrong, in Lerner's view, with financing part or all of government expenditures by the Treasury's printing of new money. According to this approach, taxes bear no relation whatsoever to expenditures. The level of spending ought to be decided upon according to the portion of total resources it is desired to devote to public in preference to private goods and services. After this issue of resource allocation has been settled, the government should

* Reprinted by permission from *Social Research* (February 1943).

19

finance them with the appropriate combination of taxing, borrowing, and printing new money entirely in terms of economic effects. Lerner also argues that if part of the expenditure is financed by borrowing, the resultant increase in public debt need cause us no concern so long as it is internally held. The repayment of principal can always be met by issuing new debt and the financing of interest by taxation involves a transfer of income among people within the country. If taxes to pay for the interest become too burdensome and restrictive on the economy, the necessary funds could even be secured by further borrowing or printing of money. If the more likely route of taxation is employed and there is an objection to the resultant redistribution of income, the tax structure can be altered to remedy this. It all returns to the fundamental point that taxation, borrowing, debt repayment, interest payments, etc., should be handled entirely with a view to their economic effects. In point of fact, Lerner contends that deficit spending and rising debt are not likely to continue indefinitely. He reasons that if the desired goal of full employment has been successfully accomplished for an extended period, investment will become more stable, and with greater personal wealth, arising from the increased holdings of government securities, the ratio of consumption to income will be larger. With this higher consumption function and more stable investment there will probably be no, or certainly less, need for further deficits and increases in debt.

APART from the necessity of winning the war, there is no task facing society today so important as the elimination of economic insecurity. If we fail in this after the war the present threat to democratic civilization will arise again. It is therefore essential that we grapple with this problem even if it involves a little careful thinking and even if the thought proves somewhat contrary to our preconceptions.

In recent years the principles by which appropriate government action can maintain prosperity have been adequately developed, but the proponents of the new principles have either not seen their full logical implications or shown an over-solicitousness which caused them to try to save the public from the necessary mental exercise. This has worked like a boomerang. Many of our publicly minded men who have come to see that deficit spending actually works still oppose the permanent maintenance of prosperity because in their failure to see *how* it all works they are easily frightened by fairy tales of terrible consequences.

I

As formulated by Alvin Hansen and others who have developed and popularized it, the new fiscal theory (which was first put forward in substantially complete form by J. M. Keynes in England) sounds a little less novel and absurd to our preconditioned ears than it does when presented in its simplest and most logical form, with all the unorthodox implications expressly formulated. In some cases the less shocking formulation may be intentional, as a tactical device to gain serious attention. In other cases it is due not to a desire to sugar the pill but to the fact that the writers themselves have not seen all the unorthodox implications — perhaps subconsciously compromising with their own orthodox education. But now it is these compromises that are under fire. Now more than ever it is necessary to pose the theorems in the purest form. Only thus will it be possible to clear the air of objections which really are concerned with awkwardnesses that appear only when the new theory is forced into the old theoretical framework.

Fundamentally the new theory, like almost every important discovery, is extremely simple. Indeed it is this simplicity which makes the public suspect it as too slick. Even learned professors who find it hard to abandon ingrained habits of thought have complained that it is "merely logical" when they could find no flaw in it. What progress the theory has made so far has been achieved not by simplifying it but by dressing it up to make it more complicated and accompanying the presentation with impressive but irrelevant statistics.

The central idea is that government fiscal policy, its spending and taxing, its borrowing and repayment of loans, its issue of new money and its withdrawal of money, shall all be undertaken with an eye only to the *results* of these actions on the economy and not to any established traditional doctrine about what is sound or unsound. This principle of judging only by *effects* has been applied in many other fields of human activity, where it is known as the method of science as opposed to scholasticism. The principle of judging fiscal measures by the way they work or function in the economy we may call *Functional Finance*.

The first financial responsibility of the government (since nobody else can undertake that responsibility) is to keep the total rate of spending in the country on goods and services neither greater nor less than that rate which at the current prices would buy all the goods that it is possible to produce. If total spending is allowed to go above this there will be inflation, and if it is allowed to go below this there will be unemployment. The government can increase total spending by spending more itself or by reducing taxes so that the taxpayers have more money left to spend. It can reduce total spending by spending less itself or by raising taxes so that taxpayers have less money left to spend. By these means total spending can be kept at the required level, where it will be enough to buy the goods that can be produced by all who want to work, and yet not enough to bring inflation by demanding (at current prices) *more* than can be produced.

In applying this first law of Functional Finance, the government may find itself collecting more in taxes than it is spending, or spending more than it collects in taxes. In the former case it can keep the difference in its coffers or use it to repay some of the national debt, and in the latter case it would have to provide the difference by borrowing or printing money. In neither case should the government feel that there is anything especially good or bad about this result; it should merely concentrate on keeping the total rate of spending neither too small nor too great, in this way preventing both unemployment and inflation.

An interesting, and to many a shocking, corollary is that taxing is *never* to be undertaken merely because the government needs to make money payments. According to the principles of Functional Finance, taxation must be judged only by its effects. Its main effects are two: the taxpayer has less money left to spend and the government has more money. The second effect can be brought about so much more easily by printing the money that only the first effect is significant. Taxation should therefore be imposed only when it is desirable that the taxpayers shall have less money to spend, for example, when they would otherwise spend enough to bring about inflation.

The second law of Functional Finance is that the government should borrow money only if it is desirable that the public should have less money and more government bonds, for these are the *effects* of government borrowing. This might be desirable if otherwise the rate of interest would be reduced too low (by attempts on the part of the holders of the cash to lend it out) and induce too much investment, thus bringing about inflation. Conversely, the government should lend money (or repay some of its debt) only if it is desirable to increase the money or to reduce the quantity of government bonds in the hands of the public. When taxing, spending, borrowing and lending (or repaying loans) are governed by the principles of Functional Finance, any excess of money outlays over money revenues, if it cannot be met out of money hoards, must be met by printing new money, and any excess of revenues over outlays can be destroyed or used to replenish hoards.

The almost instinctive revulsion that we have to the idea of printing money, and the tendency to identify it with inflation, can be overcome if we calm ourselves and take note that this printing does not affect the amount of money *spent*. That is regulated by the first law of Functional Finance, which refers especially to inflation and unemployment. The printing of money takes place only when it is needed to implement Functional Finance in spending or lending (or repayment of government debt).[1]

In brief, Functional Finance rejects completely the traditional doctrines of "sound finance" and the principle of trying to balance the budget over a solar year or any other arbitrary period. In their place it prescribes: first, the adjustment of total spending (by everybody in the economy, including the government) in order to eliminate both unemployment and inflation, using government spending when total spending is too low and taxation when total spending is too high; second, the adjustment of public holdings of money and of government bonds, by government borrowing or debt repayment, in order to achieve the rate of interest which results in the most desirable level of investment; and, third, the printing, hoarding or destruction of money as needed for carrying out the first two parts of the program.

II

In judging the formulations of economists on this subject it is difficult to distinguish between tact in smoothing over the more staggering statements of Functional Finance and insufficient clarity on the part of those who do not fully realize the extremes that are implied in their relatively orthodox formulations. First there were the pump-primers, whose argument was that the government merely had to get things going and then the economy could go on by itself. There are very few pump-primers left now. A formula similar in

---

[1] Borrowing money from the banks, on conditions which permit the banks to issue new credit money based on their additional holdings of government securities, must be considered for our purpose as printing money. In effect the banks are acting as agents for the government in issuing credit or bank money.

some ways to pump-priming was developed by Scandinavian economists in terms of a series of cyclical, capital and other special budgets which had to be balanced not annually but over longer periods. Like the pump-priming formula it fails because there is no reason for supposing that the spending and taxation policy which maintains full employment and prevents inflation must necessarily balance the budget over a decade any more than during a year or at the end of each fortnight.

As soon as this was seen — the lack of any guarantee that the maintenance of prosperity would permit the budget to be balanced even over longer periods — it had to be recognized that the result might be a continually increasing national debt (if the additional spending were provided by the government's borrowing of the money and not by printing the excess of its spending over its tax revenues). At this point two things should have been made clear: first, that this possibility presented no danger to society, no matter what unimagined heights the national debt might reach, so long as Functional Finance maintained the proper level of total demand for current output; and second (though this is much less important), that there is an automatic tendency for the budget to be balanced in the long run as a *result* of the application of Functional Finance, even if there is no place for the *principle* of balancing the budget. No matter how much interest has to be paid on the debt, taxation must not be applied unless it is necessary to keep spending down to prevent inflation. The interest can be paid by borrowing still more.

As long as the public is willing to keep on lending to the government there is no difficulty, no matter how many zeros are added to the national debt. If the public becomes reluctant to keep on lending, it must either hoard the money or spend it. If the public hoards, the government can print the money to meet its interest and other obligations, and the only effect is that the public holds government currency instead of government bonds and the government is saved the trouble of making interest payments. If the public spends, this will increase the rate of total spending so that it will not be necessary for the government to borrow for this purpose; and if the rate of spending becomes too great, *then* is the time to tax to prevent inflation. The proceeds can then be used to pay interest and repay government debt. In every case Functional Finance provides a simple, quasi-automatic response.

But either this was not seen clearly or it was considered too shocking or too logical to be told to the public. Instead it was argued, for example by Alvin Hansen, that as long as there is a reasonable ratio between national income and debt, the interest payment on the national debt can easily come from taxes paid out of the increased national income created by the deficit financing.

This unnecessary "appeasement" opened the way to an extremely effective opposition to Functional Finance. Even men who have a clear understanding of the mechanism whereby government spending in times of depression can increase the national income by several times the amount laid out by the government, and who understand perfectly well that the national debt, when it is not owed to other nations, is not a burden on the nation in the same way as an individual's debt to other individuals is a burden on the individual, have come out strongly against "deficit spending."[2] It has been argued that "it would be impossible to devise a program better adapted to the systematic undermining of the private-enterprise system and the hastening of the final catastrophe than 'deficit spending.'"[3]

These objections are based on the recognition that although every dollar spent by the government may create several dollars of income in the course of the next year or two, the effects then disappear. From this it follows that if the national income is to be maintained at a high level the government has to keep up its contribution to spending for as long as private spending is insufficient by itself to provide full employment. This might mean an indefinite continuation of government support to spending (though not necessarily at an increasing rate); and if, as the "appeasement" formulation suggests, all this spending comes out of borrowing, the debt will keep on growing until it is no longer in a "reasonable" ratio to income.

This leads to the crux of the argument. If the interest on the debt must be raised out of taxes (again an assumption that is unchallenged by the "appeasement" formulation) it will in time constitute an important fraction of the national income. The very high income tax necessary to collect this amount of money and pay it to the holders of government bonds will discourage risky private investment, by so reducing the net return on it that the investor is not compensated for the risk of losing his capital. This will make it necessary for the government to undertake still more deficit financing to keep up the level of income and employment. Still heavier taxation will then be necessary to pay the interest on the growing debt — until the burden of taxation is so crushing that private investment

[2] An excellent example of this is the persuasive article by John T. Flynn in *Harper's Magazine* for July 1942.

[3] Flynn, *ibid.*

becomes unprofitable, and the private enterprise economy collapses. Private firms and corporations will all be bankrupted by the taxes, and the government will have to take over all industry.

This argument is not new. The identical calamities, although they are now receiving much more attention than usual, were promised when the first income tax law of one penny in the pound was proposed. All this only makes it more important to evaluate the significance of the argument.

III

There are four major errors in the argument against deficit spending, four reasons why its apparent conclusiveness is only illusory.

In the first place, the same high income tax that reduces the return on the investment is deductible for the loss that is incurred if the investment turns out a failure. As a result of this the *net* return on the risk of loss is unaffected by the income tax rate, no matter how high that may be. Consider an investor in the $50,000-a-year income class who has accumulated $10,000 to invest. At 6 per cent this would yield $600, but after paying income tax on this addition to his income at 60 cents in the dollar he would have only $240 left. It is argued, therefore, that he would not invest because this is insufficient compensation for the risk of losing $10,000. This argument forgets that if the $10,000 is all lost, the net loss to the investor, after he has deducted his income tax allowance, will be only $4,000, and the rate of return on the amount he actually risks is still exactly 6 per cent; $240 is 6 per cent of $4,000. The effect of the income tax is to make the rich man act as a kind of agent working for society on commission. He receives only a part of the return on the investment, but he loses only a part of the money that is invested. Any investment that was worth undertaking in the absence of the income tax is still worth undertaking.

Of course, this correction of the argument is strictly true only where 100 per cent of the loss is deductible from taxable income, where relief from taxation occurs at the same rate as the tax on returns. There is a good case against certain limitations on permissible deduction from the income tax base for losses incurred, but that is another story. Something of the argument remains, too, if the loss would put the taxpayer into a lower income tax bracket, where the rebate (and the tax) is at a lower rate. There would then be some reduction in the net return as compared with the potential net loss. But this would apply only to such investments as are large enough to threaten to impoverish the investor if they fail. It was for the express purpose of dealing with this problem that the corporation was devised, making it possible for many individuals to combine and undertake risky enterprises without any one person having to risk all his fortune on one venture. But quite apart from corporate investment, this problem would be met almost entirely if the maximum rate of income tax were reached at a relatively low level, say at $25,000 a year (low, that is, from the point of view of the rich men who are the supposed source of risk capital). Even if all income in excess of $25,000 were taxed at 90 per cent there would be no discouragement in the investment of any part of income over this level. True, the net return, after payment of tax, would be only one-tenth of the nominal interest payments, but the amount risked by the investors would also be only ten per cent of the actual capital invested, and therefore the net return on the capital actually risked by the investor would be unaffected.

In the second place, this argument against deficit spending in time of depression would be indefensible even if the harm done by debt were as great as has been suggested. It must be remembered that spending by the government increases the *real* national income of goods and services by several times the amount spent by the government, and that the burden is measured not by the amount of the interest payments but only by the inconveniences involved in the process of transferring the money from the taxpayers to the bond-holders. Therefore objecting to deficit spending is like arguing that if you are offered a job when out of work on the condition that you promise to pay your wife interest on a part of the money earned (or that your wife pay it to you) it would be wiser to continue to be unemployed, because in time you will be owing your wife a great deal of money (or she will be owing it to you), and this might cause matrimonial difficulties in the future. Even if the interest payments were really lost to society, instead of being merely transferred within the society, they would come to much less than the loss through permitting unemployment to continue. That loss would be several times as great as the *capital* on which these interest payments have to be made.

In the third place, there is no good reason for supposing that the government would have to raise all the interest on the national debt by current taxes. We have seen that Functional Finance permits taxation only when the *direct* effect of the tax is in the social interest, as when it prevents excessive spending or excessive investment which would bring about inflation. If taxes imposed to prevent inflation do not result in sufficient proceeds, the interest on the debt can be met by borrowing or printing the money. There is no risk of inflation from this, because if there were such a risk a greater amount would have to be collected in taxes.

This means that the absolute size of the national debt does not matter at all, and that however large the interest payments that have to be made, these do not constitute any burden upon society as a whole. A completely fantastic exaggeration may illustrate the point. Suppose the national debt reaches the stupendous total of ten thousand billion dollars (that is, ten trillion, $10,000,000,000,000), so that the interest on it is 300 billion a year. Suppose the real national income of goods and services which can be produced by the economy when fully employed is 150 billion. The interest alone, therefore, comes to twice the real national income. There is no doubt that a debt of this size would be called "unreasonable." But even in this fantastic case the payment of the interest constitutes no burden on society. Although the real income is only 150 billion dollars the money income is 450 billion — 150 billion in income from the production of goods and services and 300 billion in income from ownership of the government bonds which constitute the national debt. Of this money income of 450 billion, 300 billion has to be collected in taxes by the government for interest payments (if 10 trillion is the legal debt limit), but after payment of these taxes there remains 150 billion dollars in the hands of the taxpayers, and this is enough to pay for all the goods and services that the economy can produce. Indeed it would do the public no good to have any more money left after tax payments, because if it spent more than 150 billion dollars it would merely be raising the prices of the goods bought. It would not be able to obtain more goods to consume than the country is able to produce.

Of course this illustration must not be taken to imply that a debt of this size is at all likely to come about as a result of the application of Functional Finance. As will be shown below, there is a natural tendency for the national debt to stop growing long before it comes anywhere near the astronomical figures that we have been playing with.

The unfounded assumption that current interest on the debt must be collected in taxes springs from the idea that the debt must be kept in a "reasonable" or "manageable" ratio to income (whatever that may be). If this restriction is accepted, *borrowing* to pay the interest is eliminated as soon as the limit of "reasonableness" is reached, and if we further rule out, as an indecent thought, the possibility of *printing* the money, there remains only the possibility of raising the interest payments by taxes. Fortunately there is no need to assume these limitations so long as Functional Finance is on guard against inflation, for it is the fear of inflation which is the only rational basis for suspicion of the printing of money.

Finally, there is no reason for assuming that, as a result of the continued application of Functional Finance to maintain full employment, the government must always be borrowing more money and increasing the national debt. There are a number of reasons for this.

First, full employment *can* be maintained by printing the money needed for it, and this does not increase the debt at all. It is probably advisable, however, to allow debt and money to increase together in a certain balance, as long as one or the other has to increase.

Second, since one of the greatest deterrents to private investment is the fear that the depression will come before the investment has paid for itself, the guarantee of permanent full employment will make private investment much more attractive, once investors have got over their suspicions of the new procedure. The greater private investment will diminish the need for deficit spending.

Third, as the national debt increases, and with it the sum of private wealth, there will be an increasing yield from taxes on higher incomes and inheritances, even if the tax rates are unchanged. These higher tax payments do not represent reductions of spending by the taxpayers. Therefore the government does not have to use these proceeds to maintain the requisite rate of spending, and it can devote them to paying the interest on the national debt.

Fourth, as the national debt increases it acts as a self-equilibrating force, gradually diminishing the further need for its growth and finally reaching an equilibrium level where its tendency to grow comes completely to an end. The greater the national debt the greater is the quantity of private wealth. The reason for this is simply that for every dollar of debt owed by the government there is a private creditor who owns the government obligations (possibly through a corporation in which he has shares), and who regards these obligations as part of his private fortune. The greater the private fortunes the less is the incentive to add to them by saving out of current income. As current saving is thus discouraged by the great accumulation of past savings, spending out of current income increases (since spending is the only alternative to saving income). This increase in private spending makes it less necessary for the government to undertake deficit financing to keep total spending at the level which provides full employment. When the government debt has become so great that private spending is enough to provide the total spending needed for full employment, there is no need for any deficit financing by the government, the budget is balanced and the national debt automatically stops growing. The size of this equilibrium level of debt depends on many things. It can only be guessed at, and in the very roughest manner. My guess is that it is between 100 and 300 billion dollars. Since the level is a result and not a principle of Functional Finance the latitude of such a guess does not matter; it is not needed for the application of the laws of Functional Finance.

Fifth, if for any reason the government does not wish to see private property grow too much (whether in the form of government bonds or otherwise) it can check this by taxing the rich instead of borrowing from them, in its program of financing government spending to maintain full employment. The rich will not reduce their spending significantly, and thus the effects on the economy, apart from the smaller debt, will be the same as if the money had been borrowed from them. By this means the debt can be reduced to any desired level and kept there.

The answers to the argument against deficit spending may thus be summarized as follows:

The national debt does not have to keep on increasing;

Even if the national debt does grow, the interest on it does not have to be raised out of current taxes;

Even if the interest on the debt is raised out of current taxes, these taxes constitute only the interest on only a fraction of the benefit enjoyed from the government spending, and are not lost to the nation but are merely transferred from taxpayers to bondholders;

High income taxes need not discourage investment, because appropriate deductions for losses can diminish the capital actually risked by the investor in the same proportion as his net income from the investment is reduced.

IV

If the propositions of Functional Finance were put forward without fear of appearing too logical, criticisms like those discussed above would not be as popular as they now are, and it would not be necessary to defend Functional Finance from its friends. An especially embarrassing task arises from the claim that Functional Finance (or deficit financing, as it is frequently but unsatisfactorily called) is primarily a defense of private enterprise. In the attempt to gain popularity for Functional Finance, it has been given other names and declared to be essentially directed toward saving private enterprise. I myself have sinned similarly in previous writings in identifying it with democracy,[4] thus joining the army of salesmen who wrap up their wares in the flag and tie anything they have to sell to victory or morale.

Functional Finance is not especially related to democracy or to private enterprise. It is applicable to a communist society just as well as to a fascist society or a democratic society. It is applicable to any society in which money is used as an important element in the economic mechanism. It consists of the simple principle of giving up our preconceptions of what is proper or sound or traditional, of what "is done," and instead considering the *functions* performed in the economy by government taxing and spending and borrowing and lending. It means using these instruments simply as instruments, and not as magic charms that will cause mysterious hurt if they are manipulated by the wrong people or without due reverence for tradition. Like any other mechanism, Functional Finance will work no matter who pulls the levers. Its relationship to democracy and free enterprise consists simply in the fact that if the people who believe in these things will not use Functional Finance, they will stand no chance in the long run against others who will.

GERHARD COLM

Fiscal Policy and the Federal Budget[*]

Many economists consider the preceding argument by Lerner to be an overly-optimistic view of the ease with which stable full employment can be achieved with bold implementation of fiscal policy. Among such critics is Gerhard Colm who, although in favor of discretionary

---

[4] In "Total Democracy and Full Employment," *Social Change* (May 1941).

[*] Abridged and reprinted by permission from *Income Stabilization for a Developing Democracy*, Max F. Millikan, ed. (Yale University Press, New Haven, 1953.)

use of fiscal policy for stabilization purposes, nevertheless points to a number of obstacles. In the following selection he presents an historical account of the record of fiscal policy from 1933 to 1951 and an analysis of some of the difficulties involved. The author concludes that federal deficit spending contributed to economic expansion from 1933 to 1937 but was not successful as a pump primer; when the government deficit decreased in 1937, the economy moved into a sharp decline. In the immediate post-World War II period even substantial budget surpluses were not sufficient to prevent inflation, and Colm suggests that this was due at least in part to the fact that the monetary authorities pursued an easy money policy. It will be recalled from the introduction to these readings that this resulted from their policy of supporting the government bond market. Colm also suggests that part of the difficulty confronting fiscal policy in this period, as in others, is that the inflation may have been partly caused by cost-price factors or a wage-price spiral, not by excessive demand. In sum, though, the author believes that the budget surpluses in 1947 and 1948 and again in 1950–51 helped restrain inflation while the deficit in 1948–49 contributed to a moderation of recession. Among other problems to which Colm refers are the conflicts encountered in trying to adjust tax and expenditure policies to combat short-run instability without upsetting long-run goals, and the limitation posed by legislative delay. In presenting these and other problems the author suggests remedies and remains at least moderately optimistic. Based on his examination of the historical record and analysis of the problems involved, Colm sees fiscal policy as an important and, hopefully, improving aid to economic stability, but rejects the notion that its use is as simple as implied in Lerner's theory of functional finance.

FISCAL POLICY: THE EVOLUTION OF AN IDEA

The great depression dramatized the dilemma in which Western capitalism found itself in recent decades. The free enterprise system had unleashed tremendous productive forces which carried the technical revolution from one field of production to another and from one region of the world to another. The standard of living in the industrial regions of the world showed great gains. It brought into sight an age of plenty.

On the other hand, there was a growing threat of instability. The expectation that the economic system of free enterprise and free markets would bring about steady and full utilization of all resources gave way to a growing fear that instability and periodic depressions are the price that must be paid for freedom and progress.

The earlier hopes that the government could steer an otherwise free economy solely through the device of a deliberate central bank policy were shaken by the experiences during the boom of the twenties and the depression of the thirties. Many people began to wonder whether liberal institutions and rapid and sustained economic progress were compatible with each other, or whether sacrifices with respect to one were necessary in order to gain the other.

In this situation what has come to be known as fiscal policy was proposed as a means to overcome depressions. It was greeted with enthusiasm as it promised to combine steady economic and social progress with the maintenance of basic economic liberties. It appeared as the true middle-of-the-road policy that avoided the fatal mistakes of a do-nothing policy without choosing the equally fatal policy of economic regimentation.

This is not the place to describe how this idea of fiscal policy grew out of modern theory and recent experience,[1] but a brief explanation may be in order. In its simplest form fiscal policy is conceived as a means to counteract the economic instability that is caused at times by active purchasing power exceeding the supply of goods at existing prices or at other times by the sum total of demand falling short of potential supply. If inflationary tendencies prevail, the government increases taxes or curtails expenditures, thus reducing purchasing power. In periods of deflation and underemployment the government decreases taxes and increases expenditures, thereby adding to active purchasing power and effective demand. If the government succeeds in influencing the total stream of purchasing power and active demand, production will be forthcoming in the right amount and composition, and no other government regulation is needed to stabilize the economy and promote economic growth.

Fiscal policy seemed to be the ideal tool which could repair the

[1] There is extensive literature on this topic, particularly with respect to the relationship between Keynes's theory of employment and Hansen's theory of fiscal policy. See, for instance, *The New Economics: Keynes' Influence on Theory and Public Policy*, Seymour E. Harris, ed. (New York, Knopf, 1947), and *Income, Employment, and Public Policy*, essays in honor of Alvin H. Hansen by Lloyd A. Metzler, and others (New York, Norton, 1948). Arthur Smithies has treated the subject of this chapter in "Federal Budgeting and Fiscal Policy," in *A Survey of Contemporary Economics*, Howard S. Ellis, ed. (Philadelphia, Blakiston, 1948).

basic defect in a laissez-faire economy without any specific interference with the free decisions by management of what and how to
produce, by labor where to work, and by consumers what to do with
their money. No new government powers would be needed except
an adaptation of conventional government activities, namely, collecting revenue, spending money, and managing the debt.

Like all great ideas, the concept of fiscal policy was characterized
by its simplicity. Little of that simplicity is left in present-day dis-
cussions about the actual role that fiscal policy may play in an
endeavor toward stabilization of income and employment.[2] A survey
of our experience with fiscal policy during the depression, the war
period, and the postwar and rearmament period may help to focus
on some of the problems that have been encountered in the attempt
to adopt fiscal policies as a stabilization device.

1. The Great Depression

Government expenditure and revenue policy during the great depression can only to a limited extent be regarded as a test of the effectiveness of fiscal policy. The contraction in incomes, investment, and
employment certainly called for support of purchasing power in
order to bring the downward spiral to a halt. Actually, tax rates
were not reduced but rather increased. Particularly, state and local
taxes were increased, contributions to social insurance were initiated,
and some other federal taxes were raised.

Expenditures by the federal government, on the other hand,
were increased rapidly. A large part of the emergency outlays, however, were designed to enable farmers, homeowners, and businessmen
to meet their debt obligations and to avoid bankruptcy and fore-
closure. Most of these outlays simply substituted a federal debt for a
private debt without a substantial addition to current purchasing
power. Furthermore, the effect of the increase in purchasing power
generated through federal expenditures was largely offset by the
curtailment in state-local expenditures so that the total additional
government "net contribution" to purchasing power was only of
limited size.

---

[2] The recent report on *National and International Measures for Full Employment,* submitted by a group of experts appointed by the Secretary-General of
the United Nations (December, 1949), presents a very clear though still over-
simplified exposition of these problems. (See also the discussion of this report
in the proceedings of the Eleventh Session of the Social and Economic Council
of the United Nations in Geneva, July, 1950.)

Additional government expenditures for public works create, primarily, additional income of workers and contractors on and off site; these workers and contractors spend some of their additional income and, as a secondary effect of government expenditures, incomes are created in the hands of grocers, bakers, millers, and so on. During the period of recovery, the national income increased between two and three times as much as the government net contribution. This seemed to corroborate Keynes's theory of a "multiplier" — if one ascribes much of the recovery in national income to the effect of government expenditures, which is not an unreasonable assumption for this period.[3]

The concept of pump-priming, which was used during those years, implied, however, more than this multiplier. The pump-priming theory held that the increase in consumer purchasing power and demand would induce a genuine revival of business investment. To the extent that investment began to rise, it was hoped that the recovery movement would continue under its own momentum and that the government net contribution could be safely reduced or discontinued. Investment, however, rose only very moderately, not enough to carry the recovery movement forward under its own steam. Thus the pump-priming or the "acceleration" effect of government spending did not materialize to a sufficient extent. The recovery movement did not become self-sustaining. As a matter of fact, a reduction in the government's net contribution to purchasing power in 1937 coincided with the beginning of a serious recession.

In response to the 1937–38 recession, the first systematic plan of fiscal policy for purposes of stabilization was devised by the administration, but only partly adopted by Congress. There was still considerable unemployment when the defense effort began to supersede the recovery effort.[4]

This incomplete success of the government's fiscal policy in

[3] For an attempt to classify government expenditures according to their effect on national income and capital, and for an attempt to measure the effect of such expenditures, see Gerhard Colm and Fritz Lehmann, "Public Spending and Recovery in the United States," *Social Research*, 3 (May, 1936).

[4] The 1937–38 recession and revival offers excellent material for a study of fiscal policy. Extremely interesting is Marriner Eccles' dramatic story of these events in his memoirs, *Beckoning Frontiers* (New York, Knopf, 1951). A valuable analysis of the possible causal relationship between these events is given by Kenneth D. Roose in "The Role of Net Contribution to Income in the Recession and Revival of 1937–38," *Journal of Finance*, 6, No. 1 (March, 1951).

inducing a self-supporting recovery movement has been attributed, first of all, to the fact that the size of the net contribution was not large enough. While emphasis was on additional expenditures, taxes were increased. A combination of tax reduction and increased expenditures would probably have exerted a greater effect on purchasing power and business investment.

Reflecting upon the consequences a different policy might have had during the depression, one should not forget to take the mores of the time into consideration. The majority of the people demanded bold leadership and appreciated the pursuit of new types of policies. It is difficult to say, however, whether a still bolder policy would have frightened people and created a negative economic effect. Nevertheless, irrespective of what could have been done during the thirties, it is important to recognize now that the size of the *net* contribution of the government to purchasing power probably was not adequate to offset the strong deflationary tendency.

Perhaps even more important the policy of the depression period was not exclusively or mainly a recovery policy. Under the circumstances of the period it had to be a reform policy also. As such it antagonized large sectors of business and created a climate that was unfavorable to the resumption of business investment.

Finally, the business community did not expect the recovery policy to last very long. Before each election it expected a change in administration and basic policy and waited for a political change before embarking on economic expansion.[5]

Thus it can be concluded from the experience of the thirties that an effective fiscal policy:

a) Must bring about changes in taxes and expenditures of sufficient size to restore purchasing power to the level at which business investments are forthcoming.

b) Must be coordinated with other nonfiscal policies in order to avoid self-defeating inconsistencies in policy.

c) Must be coordinated with state and local policy to prevent local policy from counteracting national policy.

d) Must be regarded as a policy that has such general popular support among various groups of the population that it can be

[5] A comparison of the attitude of business during the recovery of the thirties with that during the recovery of late 1949 and early 1950 demonstrates dramatically the influence of the "confidence" factor. The importance of this factor has been brought out in the *Fourth Annual Report to the President* by the Council of Economic Advisers, December, 1949.

expected to be continued in one form or another, irrespective of the party in power, as long as it is needed.

These are some of the lessons which can be learned from the experience of the depression of the thirties. In addition, the failure of the government-spending and deficit policy of the depression to lead to self-sustained prosperity gave rise to a discussion of the impact of a government stabilization policy on the federal debt. Under the pump-priming concept, the deficits incurred during the period of slackening private activities should be offset by surpluses during the subsequent periods of self-sustained prosperity. The budget could be balanced, if not each year, then over the cycle, that is, over a period of several years. In this case no permanent increase in the national debt would follow from the use of fiscal policy as a stabilization device.

The experience of the depression did not confirm this notion. Nevertheless the failure of government deficits to initiate a period of renewed self-sustained prosperity suggested to Alvin Hansen[6] and others that fiscal policy had to serve not merely as a temporary anticyclical device but possibly had a more permanent active role to play in promoting economic conditions of steady growth.

In line with Keynes's theory, it was argued that the economy is in balance if total demand equals, and grows in proportion to, total potential supply using all available resources. People either directly purchase goods and services for their personal consumption or save. Net saving by individuals or corporate business offsets outlays for producers' goods such as plant and equipment, tools, residential houses,[7] commercial buildings, and other investments. The economy is in balance on a high level of activity if the amounts persons and corporations wish to put aside as savings are equal to the amounts persons and corporations wish to use for investment. In that case the sum of direct consumer and indirect business demand is equal to the potential output, and the economy proceeds on a full employment level. Hansen maintains that there is at least the possibility that in a "mature" economy the amount people and business managers wish to save from full employment incomes and profits may be larger

[6] Alvin Hansen, *Fiscal Policy and Business Cycles* (New York, Norton, 1941).

[7] Construction of residential houses is regarded as investment and the use of the houses as a consumer service. It has been found statistically convenient to treat all residential housing as if it were built for rental purposes even though in the case of owner-occupied houses the landlord and the tenant are identical persons.

than the amounts they wish to invest — year in, year out — through additions to their plant and equipment, inventories, houses, or foreign investments. As long as that is the case we have the threat of a downdrift in economic activity.

Such a tendency of potential oversaving or underinvestment could be counteracted, for example, by tax legislation that curtails saving more than spending, or by public investment that supplements private investment. In order to be most effective some part of this public investment should be financed by government borrowing, so that the government would put into active use some of the nation's saving that is forthcoming at a high and rising level in income and profit.

This concept leaves at least the possibility that a compensatory fiscal policy may lead to a permanent increase in the absolute size of the national debt. According to Evsey Domar[8] and others this does not mean a necessarily increasing debt *burden*. The burden of the debt is determined by the interest rate charged and its relationship to taxable incomes. If private and public investment result in a steady expansion of productivity and income, the tax base grows more than the interest the government has to pay on the debt (particularly if a part of the new issues are placed with the central banking system at nominal interest rates). A moderate permanent net addition to the debt over the cycle, such as might be needed to balance the nation's saving and investment on a level of high and expanding activity, would not necessarily be a cause for alarm.

This debate was in full swing when the relatively limited spending programs for recovery gave way to the large-scale programs for defense and war spending. The issues were not solved but postponed for the time being; and the much-discussed depression debt was dwarfed by the huge increase in debt that resulted from the war.

2. World War II

While a concept of fiscal policy only gradually emerged from the experience of the depression, the financing of World War II was considered from the beginning in the light of its possible contribution to economic mobilization and stabilization.

At the beginning of the defense program the President recommended only moderate tax increases in order to permit an expansion of economic activities and absorption of unemployment. At the

---

[8] Evsey Domar, "The 'Burden of the Debt' and National Income," *American Economic Review*, 34 (December, 1944), 798–827.

same time less essential public works and work relief were drastically reduced in order to channel employment into essential lines of industry.[9] With the stepping-up of the defense and war program, the President recommended a drastic tax program with sharper tax increases than Congress was ready to adopt.[10] The recommended tax increases, and particularly those that were enacted, could absorb only a part of the inflationary gap that had resulted from the creation of incomes far in excess of available goods left for civilian use.

Economic stabilization during the war had to rely largely on nonfiscal methods of control, particularly price and wage controls, allocations, and rationing. Tax increases, however, reduced the inflationary gap so that the task to be performed by nonfiscal stabilization devices became manageable.

Two main lessons were learned from the wartime experience with fiscal policy:

a) Some further increase in taxes, and particularly the use of compulsory saving, would have made the wartime stabilization more effective and would have reduced some of the postwar difficulties. Nevertheless, fiscal measures sufficient to accomplish stabilization with lesser use of nonfiscal controls would have had to be so drastic that the tax rates would probably have interfered with incentives to work.[11] It is possible that a much more drastic tax policy would have been feasible only if a system of national service had been adopted so that there was less need to rely on income incentives.

Furthermore, fiscal policy alone would have been a very blunt instrument for curtailing the demand for scarce goods. In the light of the limited possibilities of shifting resources from one use to another, shortages in various products or services were very uneven. A carefully devised tax program could have curtailed various types of consumption in different degrees. Nevertheless, as serious wartime scarcities made it necessary to husband available resources and to

---

[9] See the *Budget Message of the President,* January 3, 1941.

[10] See the *Budget Messages of the President,* January, 1942, and the following years.

[11] At very high tax levels the same tax measure may, on the one hand, absorb purchasing power and thereby have a deflationary effect and, on the other hand, impair incentives to produce or induce cost (e.g., wage) increases and thereby have a price-raising effect. Only a case-by-case analysis can determine the point at which the price-raising effect of a tax measure begins to outweigh the deflationary effect. It is not likely that this point of diminishing anti-inflationary effect of taxes was reached under the tax rates that were adopted in the United States during the war.

channel them into the most urgent use, wartime fiscal policies had to be supplemented by nonfiscal measures of control such as allocations, rationing, price and wage controls.

b) The wartime experiences made it abundantly clear that it is important to consider changes not only in the net government contribution but also in the type of expenditures or taxes that are to be changed, and that direct as well as indirect effects of fiscal measures must be considered.

It was recognized, for instance, that taxes imposed on the masses of consumers would be most effective in limiting demand. Such tax increases, however, may make the pressure for wage increases irresistible, and these wage increases may nullify the fiscal effect of the tax increase. A compulsory saving program might have been more desirable in this respect than very drastic income or excise taxes imposed on people in the lower brackets. Curtailment of profits, on the other hand, did not have a very great direct effect on active demand but it had a restraining influence on wage demands. Even the moderate wage controls of the war period would hardly have been politically feasible without a drastic limitation of profits through taxation and renegotiation of war contracts.

Thus economic stabilization during the war required not only an increase in taxes and limitation of the budget deficit but a careful consideration of the direct and indirect effects of the specific tax devices that were used.

3. The Postwar Period

Most fiscal analysts who speculated about postwar problems during the war expected that, after a transitory period of postwar inflation, lack of purchasing power and deflation would again be our major problems.[12] It has been suggested that the government's willingness to remove controls rapidly after the war and to discontinue the

[12] I do not intend to discuss here the various errors in forecasting that were made. A few economists in this country and some foreign observers expected a depression to begin immediately after the end of major military operations. Most economists, however, expected a period of postwar inflation that would follow brief and temporary "frictional" unemployment immediately after demobilization and cancellation of war contracts. Postwar inflation has lasted longer than most economists expected. But it should be remembered that all statements about the probable postwar development were predicated on the assumption of a true peacetime budget and not on budgets that reflected high and increasing international tensions. See Michael Sapir, "Review of Economic Forecasts for the Transition Period," in *Studies in Income and Wealth* (New York, National Bureau of Economic Research, 1949), *11.*

excess profits tax must be partly attributed to the erroneous expectation of a postwar depression.

The business advocates of decontrol and tax reduction, on the other hand, based their case not on an expected depression but argued that these measures would increase the incentives for more production and would combat inflation by increasing supplies. They grossly exaggerated the degree by which tax reduction and decontrol would stimulate production.

I believe that the decision to remove controls quickly was influenced more by the belief that it would be good politics to get rid of unpopular measures as rapidly as possible rather than pursue an antidepression or an anti-inflation policy.

Nevertheless, it is very likely that different fiscal policies would have been recommended if the growing international tension and the intensity and duration of postwar inflation had been correctly foreseen. The fact remains that erroneous forecasts were very detrimental to the cause of fiscal policy in the long run.

The administration began its systematic drive for new anti-inflation measures in 1947, after a tense world situation made it clear that the postwar reduction in defense expenditures could not be continued and that substantial programs for foreign economic and military aid would have to be adopted. What was actually accomplished was a delay in the adoption of further tax cuts until 1948.

For a short time very large surpluses of federal cash receipts over payments were achieved. The cash surplus in the calendar year 1947 amounted to almost $6 billion. During the first half of the calendar year 1948 it was running at an annual rate of $12.5 billion, but later in 1948 the surplus declined under the impact of the tax reduction granted through the Revenue Act of 1948 and the rising trend of federal expenditures. Under the impact of the recession in 1949 the surplus was transformed into deficits, which lasted until the outbreak of hostilities in Korea stimulated economic activity and again created growing budget surpluses in the second half of the year 1950 and the first half of 1951.

The large cash surplus of the years 1947 and 1948 probably was one of the factors that helped to limit the inflationary pressure. More surprising is the fact that a surplus reaching at times an annual rate of more than $12 billion did not cause an actual contraction of the whole economy. If economists had been asked in previous years what the economic effect of even a temporary $12 billion budget surplus would be, most of them, I am sure, would have answered that it would throw the economy into a downward spiral. In explaining the relatively mild effect of this very large surplus, three facts ought to be considered:

a) The effectiveness of a budget surplus as an anti-inflationary device depends not only on the types of revenues that are being collected but also on the type of monetary and credit policy that is associated with the budget surplus. Actually, the credit policy of these years mitigated and partially offset the anti-inflationary effect of the budget surplus.[13] The anti-inflationary effect of fiscal and credit policies is also reduced when business is able to use liquid assets and retained profits for financing its expansion and working capital needs.

b) To the extent that the budget surplus resulted from the inflationary increase in incomes and profits, it mitigated the inflationary impact but could not reverse it.

c) A budget surplus may be effective in absorbing excess purchasing power, but it is less effective in counteracting inflationary pressure that works through the wage-price spiral. The inflationary movement of the postwar years cannot be explained solely by the fact that large spending created excess purchasing power; the size of the inflationary price rise must be explained to some extent by the fact that an initial price rise induced wage demands and that the wage increases in turn were translated into further price increases, and so on. This process, it is true, could work only as long as money and credit resources were sufficient to support the rising price level. Nevertheless, fiscal policy is not an effective device for counteracting a wage-price spiral. The "inflationary bias which may be characteristic of a high employment economy of the future is likely to operate largely from the cost and price rather than from the demand side. This possibility certainly limits the effectiveness of fiscal policy as a stabilization device and requires the use of other supplementary policies."[14]

d) The simplified concept of fiscal policy assumed that budgetary changes are the most powerful causal factors in economic development. Budgetary changes, however, are not only causes but also results of developments in the private economy. In the post-Korean period powerful inflationary pressure originated in the private sector

[13] Recognition of the fact that credit policy in part offset the anti-inflationary effect of the budgetary surplus does not mean that another credit policy would have been feasible or desirable.

[14] See Hearings on the January, 1950, *Economic Report of the President* before the Joint Committee on the Economic Report, January 17–20, 1950, p. 72.

of the economy,[15] resulting in budget surpluses. This effect was reinforced by the increase in taxes adopted promptly after the Korean outbreak. It appears likely that the budget surplus in 1950–51 has mitigated the inflationary pressure, but it was not powerful enough to prevent it. Nevertheless, the increase in taxes was probably one of the factors that aided in halting the inflationary price rise early in 1951.

Postwar experience also demonstrated that changes in the budgetary situation alone are not always a sufficient means for avoiding a recession. The government cash surplus declined from $12 to $3 billion (annual rate) from the first to the second half of the calendar year 1948.[16] This drastic change in the budgetary situation did not prevent the development of conditions which led to the recession in 1949. The change in the budgetary position was due in part to the reduction in income tax rates which largely affected taxpayers in the high income brackets and did not have a substantial impact either on mass consumption or business investment. To the extent that the decline in the cash surplus was due to an increase in government expenditures, it certainly added to the support of the economy and the mildness of the subsequent recession.

The recession of the first half of the year 1949 was characterized by a sharp decline in manufacturing production and a drastic change from inventory accumulation to inventory liquidation. Incomes and sales, however, dropped much less. The President, in his Midyear Economic Report of July, 1949, recognized the changes in the economic outlook that had taken place since his previous report of January, 1949. Recessionary forces had been developing, but it appeared likely that the sharp curtailment in orders and inventories without a corresponding decline in sales would lead to an early recovery without large-scale government interference. The President's fiscal recommendations were adapted to this analysis. He withdrew his earlier request for large tax increases and recommended a limited reduction in especially harmful excise taxes. Thus he accepted a budget deficit as an undesirable but unavoidable fact, pointing out that any attempt to balance the budget either by increasing taxes or slashing expenditure programs would aggravate the recessionary forces and might result in still larger deficits.

---

[15] It should be remembered, however, that the increase in consumer and business demand following the outbreak in Korea and the Chinese intervention took place in anticipation of rising defense expenditures and resulting shortages.

[16] *Midyear Economic Report of the President,* July, 1949, p. 45.

The President emphasized, on the other hand, that as long as economic activities were still high and market adjustments still had a chance of raising the level of activity, additional large-scale increases in government programs and large-scale tax reductions would be premature. However, government cash payments rose further, partly because of the "automatic" increase in transfer payments to farmers and the unemployed. At the same time the tax yield declined and cushioned the drop in disposable profits and incomes. The cash deficit in government (federal, state, and local) operations of $2.5 billion in 1949 and $3.4 billion in the first half of 1950 (annual rate) was probably not the sole or main factor, but it was at least a contributing factor in halting the decline and supporting the recovery movement. While the recovery movement did not restore a full employment level of national income up to the beginning of 1950, it can be assumed that the shift in the budget helped to mitigate the impact of the recession.

The role that fiscal and budgetary policies played in counteracting inflation and recession in the postwar period still remains to be analyzed in detail. What evidence we have permits, however, some tentative conclusions.

During the thirties it was thought by some economists that the government net contribution, which is essentially the cash deficit or cash surplus, was one of the main causal factors in the economy influencing the generation or contraction of purchasing power, but the experience of recent years has demonstrated that a surplus or deficit per se is not a factor sufficient to explain movements in aggregate incomes or in employment. An analysis of the nature of the changes in government transactions and in the private sectors of the economy is necessary before any conclusion can be drawn as to the causal relationship between changes in the government surplus or deficit and changes in the economy as a whole.

Government not only adds or deducts purchasing power in general but in specific ways affects personal incomes and expenditures, business profits and investments, and international transactions. Government activities may promote or impair dynamic processes developing in the private economy. Government policies, therefore, should be viewed in the light of all the factors which in their interplay make for a steadily growing economic life.

With respect to the dynamic influence of government programs the "program effect" and the "spending effect" should be distinguished. The program effect of a road program, for instance, refers to the effects of the new roads on costs of transportation of farm products or on the tourist trade and the automobile industry. The spending effect of the same program refers to the wages and profits created in the hands of construction workers and the construction industry and the secondary effects resulting from the spending of these wages and profits. Only the spending effect is usually referred to in fiscal policy considerations.

Moreover, changes may originate in consumer demand or business investments or international transactions, which in turn affect government budgets. Traffic between the public and the private sector of the economy moves not on a one-way but on a two-way street. In other words the effects of government budgets must be analyzed in the whole of the Nation's Economic Budget. Stating this prerequisite of effective fiscal policy is easier than pursuing it. Indeed, the interrelationship between public and private economic action is an area in which extensive further research is required.

Recent experience has suggested one final important lesson with respect to the idea of fiscal policy. The original prescription was simply that fiscal policy was to offset either a clearly inflationary or deflationary situation. Conditions, however, are not always of such a character that the conventional concepts of inflation and deflation can be used adequately to describe actual economic conditions or the economic outlook.

At the beginning of 1950, for instance, unemployment rose while economic conditions appeared to be almost booming. With the available resources, a considerably higher volume of goods and services could have been produced. Yet general economic conditions were not of a nature that suggested an antideflationary fiscal policy as a desirable remedy. There are situations which call for adjustments in prices and costs, and in the rate of investment and consumption, rather than for changes in fiscal policy. Such adjustments involve more than merely the absorption of or the addition to purchasing power as it is needed to compensate for inflationary or deflationary processes that are clearly under way.

At the beginning of 1950 the economy was in the process of shifting from a postwar catching-up boom to a sustainable peacetime prosperity pattern. But again the problem of the necessary long-run adjustment was postponed by the worsening of the international situation and the attack on South Korea. Again economic policy had to be oriented toward aiding a mobilization program and combating the threat of inflation. The problems of a deficiency in purchasing power moved further into the background and were overshadowed by those of allocation of resources to the most pressing needs. The urgency of defense procurement gave emphasis to a more general shift in the problem of the postwar era as compared with the depression and recovery period of the thirties. During the thirties, attention was focused on the actual or threatening lack of demand to match the increasing power to produce. Only gradually people began to realize the tremendous amount of production that would be needed to develop and conserve natural resources, modernize the productive plant of the nation, provide decent homes, and meet the demand of consumers that is forthcoming from a more nearly equal distribution of incomes. To this was added after the war the need to make a contribution to reconstruction abroad and to economic expansion in the underdeveloped areas of the world. The problem has been shifting from the creation of outlets for production to one of mobilizing productive resources and channeling output into the most urgent usages. While both these aspects of the problem may, to some extent, exist at the same time, the shift in emphasis from one to the other has important consequences for the task of fiscal policy.

4. Conclusion: A Modified Concept of Fiscal Policy

From fifteen years' experience with fiscal policy, the following conclusions can be drawn:

a) Fiscal policy, a combination of deliberate changes in expenditure programs, revenue and tax programs, and debt management policies, is well suited to aid in counteracting general inflationary or general deflationary tendencies.

b) The fiscal policy of the federal government must take into account, and must be coordinated with, the fiscal policies of state and local governments.

c) Fiscal and nonfiscal policies must be coordinated so that they complement each other and do not act at cross purposes.

d) Inflationary and deflationary tendencies may result from economic maladjustments in the price-wage-profit or investment-consumption relationship. A policy that is suitable to combat an inflationary or a deflationary movement may not remove the maladjustments that cause these movements. It is desirable to use fiscal and other policies to iron out the maladjustments before they lead to inflationary or deflationary movements.

e) If maladjustments have not been prevented in time and lead to inflationary or deflationary movements, then fiscal policies should be used at least as a temporary stabilizing device until more basic adjustment policies have been worked out. Fiscal policies are not adequate devices for combating the inflationary bias which may occur under a full employment policy.

f) The effectiveness of fiscal policy is increased when the community understands its working and has confidence in (and therefore anticipates) its results.

g) Fiscal policy must be related to the long-range requirements of allocation of resources to improvement in the standard of living, to expansion of the productive plant of the nation, to adequate defense needs, and to aid economic development abroad. Emphasis on each of these objectives varies, depending on the foremost needs of each period in the life of the nation.

There is no doubt that the task of fiscal policy, as indicated in these conclusions, is much more complex than is suggested by the simple formula proposed in "functional finance." Recognition of this complexity does not imply, however, that fiscal policy is unimportant. While sustained and steady growth of income and employment and a rational allocation of resources cannot be achieved through fiscal policy alone, it is equally true that these objectives can best be achieved with the aid of fiscal policy in a political and economic system that tries to give widest scope to individual responsibility and initiative and to minimize direct regulatory action of the government. . . .

IMPLEMENTING FISCAL POLICY THROUGH THE BUDGETARY PROCESS

The idea of fiscal policy, as sketched in the first section, has a short-run and long-run aspect. In the short-run it is the adaptation of government expenditure, revenue, and debt policies to the task of offsetting fluctuations in private activities. In the long-run aspect it involves the use of the same policies for the purpose of promoting self-sustained growth of the economy, thereby reducing the instability that causes cyclical fluctuations. Fiscal policy as a cyclical compensating device and, even more, as a long-run stabilizing device must be supplemented by other means of economic policy. Fiscal policy must be realized largely through budgetary procedures and budget policy must be related to the national economic objectives. . . .

In this section there will be presented a survey of actual or apparent conflicts between fiscal consideration and other considerations that enter into the content and operation of the budget. Some suggestions will be offered for possible reconciliation of conflicting objectives and institutions. It must be recognized, however, that not all conflicts can be resolved and that the need to compromise between various objectives of policy will remain one of the characteristics of day-by-day fiscal operations.

1. Conflict of Objectives: Economic versus Noneconomic Objectives

The size of the federal budget and major changes in it are controlled largely by what we may term noneconomic programs of the government. All programs of the government have, of course, political, social, and economic aspects. The aspect of foreign policy is predominant, for instance, in programs for national security and foreign policy. These programs, though "noneconomic" in their origin and purpose, are obviously "economic" in their impact, and the determination of their size is of course not exempt from economic consideration. In the 1950 pre-Korean budget, for instance, four major programs of the government — national defense, international commitments, veterans' programs, and interest on the public debt — required almost three-fourths of the budget total. All other activities of the federal government devoted to social welfare, health, natural resources, including atomic energy, agriculture, transportation, communications, housing, education, labor, finance, commerce and industry, and the costs of general government absorbed about $12 billion or approximately one-fourth of the budget.[17]

The international situation forced the government to step up defense and foreign aid programs while private business was engaged in a postwar investment boom. But obviously expenditures for purposes of foreign policy could not be delayed until the postwar boom began to peter out or until defense and foreign aid or veterans' programs could be fitted nicely into a compensatory fiscal policy. Obviously fiscal policy has to be adjusted to the necessity of these national objectives rather than having these national programs determined in a way that fits into a policy of economic stabilization. . . .

2. Conflict of Short-range versus Long-range Economic Policies

A possible conflict of objectives exists not only with respect to economic versus noneconomic objectives but also within the field of economic objectives itself. During the postwar years the federal

[17] *Budget Message of the President for the Fiscal Year 1950*, January, 1949.

government deferred many public works and social programs although there was no question about their long-range desirability. The longer the postwar boom lasted and the longer the policy of deferment was continued the more voices were heard which questioned that policy. It has been pointed out that it would be absurd to defer, for instance, urgently needed school buildings while building materials are being used for commercial construction of lesser social urgency. Similarly, it would be absurd to defer construction of hydroelectric power facilities if a real power shortage is a bottleneck in the expansion of needed supplies such as aluminum. . . .

In practical political terms the reconciliation between short-run and long-run objectives of economic and social policy does not appear impossible. In a dynamic society there will always be desirable new economic and social programs, or an expansion of existing programs, in the discussion stage. In prosperous times there should certainly be no absolute embargo against the adoption and expansion of economically and socially urgent government programs. Under conditions of full employment, the merits of additional programs must be such that they are clearly preferred to private programs with which they may compete for labor and material. They also require financing by additional taxes designed so as to work as an effective brake on private activity. Under depressed conditions, the tempo in the adoption of needed programs can be speeded up. Their relative costs then are lower, measured in terms of government cost accounting, tax burdens, and social accounting. It may be difficult to accomplish an expansion and contraction in government expenditures depending on the ups and downs in private activities. There is, however, such a large backlog of highly desirable improvement programs that it is feasible to plan for faster progress in periods of slackening business conditions and to hold to a somewhat slower progress as long as business activity remains high. In the postwar years we had a tremendous backlog of work to be done in housing and urban redevelopment, in transportation, educational and health facilities, and the development and conservation of national resources. Only very inadequate progress has been made on these programs during the postwar inflation. The rearmament program again forced postponement of many desirable projects. They can be developed as soon as we have passed the peak of defense preparations, serving short-run requirements by pursuing long-run needs.

Only if desirable and needed programs are prepared in advance and ready for adoption will an administration be able to resist the demand for less desirable emergency programs in case of a depression.

There is the danger that in case of a depression pressure for all kinds of payments will develop. It is true that for the immediate impact on demand a quick outpouring of money is more important than a careful selection of projects. For the long-run effect, however, it is very important that additions to expenditures be truly productive. If they add to productivity and thereby to the future tax base, they will be self-liquidating in the broadest sense of the term.

3. *Conflict of Short-range versus Long-range Tax Policies*

Every argument which limits the use of short-run variations in the rate of government expenditures becomes an argument for exploring the desirability of short-run variations in tax policy for purposes of economic stabilization. In this area too we run into a conflict of objectives.

Some statements made by A. P. Lerner and Beardsley Ruml have suggested that it is the main purpose of a national tax policy to regulate the flow of purchasing power. Taxes should be low enough to permit the purchase of everything that can be produced and high enough to prevent inflation.[18] If that were the sole or the main purpose of taxes, then our tax system and, even more, our tax ideals should be basically revised. Then the most effective taxes would be those that have the greatest direct bearing on consumption because their reduction would free purchasing power and their increase would absorb purchasing power much more effectively than any change in progressive taxes. There would really be no ground for maintaining progressive taxes in the tax system.

Obviously, tax policy, no less than expenditure policy, must consider other long-run economic and social objectives as well as price stabilization. A wartime experience may be mentioned to illustrate a possible conflict between these objectives. When an anti-inflationary fiscal program was under discussion during the war, a modified sales tax was suggested for consideration. The tax proposal was devised so that the buyer could obtain refunds in bonds or

---

[18] See, for example, A. P. Lerner, *Economics of Control* (New York, Macmillan, 1944), ch. 24. Reference is made to Lerner because the position he takes in the work referred to is the most uncompromising and therefore particularly suitable for an argument about the principles. See also various statements by Beardsley Ruml, such as, ". . . our taxes should be as low as they possibly can be without putting the value of our money in danger of inflation." National Tax Association, *Proceedings of the 37th Annual Conference* (1944), p. 167. Both authors have recognized other specific purposes of taxation and the need for nonbudgetary devices for stabilization.

cash on a per capita minimum of taxable purchases. Such exemption was believed necessary for reasons of equity and in order to reduce the effect of the tax on wage demands which would have nullified much of its anti-inflationary impact. Nevertheless, the proposal was turned down because of the opinion that a sales tax once admitted to the family of respectable federal taxes would probably be retained even at a time when the specific fiscal argument was no longer applicable.

In expenditure and tax policy those measures are best that reconcile the requirements of both short-run and long-run policy objectives.

4. *Conflict in Jurisdiction: Federal versus State and Local Programs*

One of the definite lessons to be derived from the experience of the great depression and the war and postwar period is that an effective fiscal policy cannot be limited to the operations of the federal government alone.

State and local financial policies tend to aggravate rather than to counteract cyclical fluctuations. During the depression state and local governments were forced to curtail expenditures and to raise tax rates. One scheme after another was devised to aid state and local undertakings — with only partial success and much criticism. Without the various aid programs curtailment of state and local services would have been much more drastic.

During the war ample revenues and the limitations on spending (because of physical restrictions) created budgetary surpluses and temptations to reduce tax rates. Tax reductions could be kept within limits because many governors and state legislatures responded to the appeal for voluntary state cooperation in the national anti-inflation program. After the war, when the appeal to cooperate in a national program of anti-inflationary fiscal policy was less effective, state and local bodies rapidly spent much of their wartime surpluses and contributed substantially to the inflationary pressure. The absence of federal-state-local coordinating machinery constitutes one of the most serious limitations on an effective national fiscal policy.

A possible step toward such coordination might consist in the establishment of flexible grants-in-aid. The federal government pays about $2.5 billion per year to state and local governments in the form of grants for a variety of purposes. That is about 6% of the federal budget but almost 15% of state and local receipts.

An element of flexibility could be introduced into the federal-state-local relationship if the federal government were to contribute a lower percentage of state-local outlays as grants for specific programs in booms and a higher percentage in depressions.[19] Although such flexibility provisions may not be feasible in the case of all programs, they do appear feasible in some and could at least contribute to the prevention of cyclically "perverse" fluctuations in state-local spending. Beyond that, at least in the case of some programs, such provisions might induce countercyclical timing of expenditures even at the state and local level.

Flexible grants-in-aid for state and local public works might be a useful instrument for building up a "shelf" of state and local public works projects. The trouble with a shelf of public works is that as soon as worthwhile projects are prepared in blueprints, local pressures become active urging their immediate execution, irrespective of the business situation. An incentive for a more reasonable policy could be created if the federal government would pay nothing or merely make a nominal contribution to such projects when undertaken in times of prosperity, but a larger percentage contribution when conditions are less favorable. . . .

5. Conflict in Procedures: Requirements of Legislative Control versus the Need for Flexibility of Government Expenditures and Revenues

The budget procedure was developed . . . as a means of legislative control of government operations. The legislative machinery with its committee setup and public hearings is not designed for quick action except in cases of obvious emergency. Appropriation and tax legislation must usually be initiated a considerable time before the expenditures are to be made or tax changes become effective. For stabilization purposes, on the other hand, it is necessary that fiscal policy be adaptable quickly to short-run changes in the economic situation.

From the point of view of fiscal policy, it would be most desirable if the executive branch were given the authority to change the rate of expenditures within given statutory limits in the same manner in which the Federal Reserve System, for instance, is authorized to

[19] See the Report of the Joint Committee on the Economic Report, March, 1949, pp. 37–38. For a detailed discussion see James A. Maxwell, *Federal Grants and the Business Cycle* (New York, National Bureau of Economic Research, 1952).

change reserve requirements within certain limits. Such delegation of authority obviously must be reconciled with the purpose of legislative control. A workable democracy requires that both the legislature and the executive share in the responsibility for stabilization policy. Thus some reconciliation between the objectives of fiscal flexibility and of legislative control must be worked out. . . .[20]

A possible way of reconciling the goal of legislative control with that of executive discretion would be to distinguish three types of expenditures in the budget. One type would include current operations of the government for which appropriations would be made on a strictly annual basis.

A second type of expenditure would be for public works and economic development. Appropriations for these purposes would be made, let us say, on a five-year basis, with executive discretion to vary the speed of program execution in line with economic requirements. In order to preserve the desirable legislative controls, it could be provided that the program be subject to annual legislative consideration for the subsequent five years, and that each year the President should report if actual obligations or expenditures in any one year fall considerably short of or considerably exceed the obligations or expenditures which were scheduled for that particular year under the five-year program.[21]

In a third type of expenditures, the quasi-commercial outlays of government corporations, the greatest degree of administrative discretion should be permitted. Like the Reconstruction Finance Corporation or the Tennessee Valley Authority, they should be authorized to adapt their activities promptly to changes in economic conditions. While these agencies should be free of too specific legislative direc-

[20] See G. L. Bach, "Monetary-Fiscal Policy Reconsidered," *Journal of Political Economy,* 57, No. 5 (October, 1949), p. 387: "But to assume congressional renunciation of direct control over the power to tax and the power to spend, except possibly for some delegation of authority over timing of prearranged programs, appears to have little relevance to reality. Formulation of a workable monetary-fiscal policy must recognize the stubborn fact of congressional prerogatives."

[21] See Harold D. Smith, *op. cit.,* pp. 96 ff. See also Gerhard Colm, "Comment on Extraordinary Budgets," *Social Research,* 5 (May, 1938), 168 ff. Of interest is the provision in the Housing Act of 1949 which authorizes a six-year program of 810,000 units of public low-cost housing, or 135,000 a year, but permits the President, after receiving advice from the Council of Economic Advisers, to vary the number of starts for any of the six years to between 50,000 and 200,000. Even though this provision had no practical consequence, it may well be regarded as a significant landmark in economic legislation.

tion, they should be geared into a national development and stabilization program. It has been the experience in many countries that the directors of government corporations often want to be "masters in their own houses" just as much if not more than directors in private corporations. In other words the activities of government corporations must effectively be made subject to executive control, without depriving "business-type" operations of the government of the desirable flexibility. . . .

Recently, proposals have been made to introduce formula flexibility into the tax system by providing for changes in tax rates when an index of production or unemployment (or any combination of indices) indicates that a substantial change in economic activities has taken place.[22]

While very good arguments in favor of formula flexibility have been advanced, there are probably more valid reasons against adoption of that plan under present circumstances. First of all, we know too little about what kind and amount of tax change would be called for when unemployment has reached a certain point. Much more fiscal policy by trial and error will be needed before we are ready to crystallize a definite scheme of flexibility in legislation.

Second, legislation must consider a variety of objectives and, depending on the particular circumstances, different tax measures may be needed in conditions which appear statistically similar. Formula flexibility may not be flexible enough.

Third, formula flexibility assumes that short-run changes in tax rates can be entirely separated from the changes which are in the long-range interest in an improved tax system. If a situation calls for tax reductions, those will be most desirable which will aid in the immediate situation and at the same time be justified as a long-run improvement of the tax system.

Finally, legislative prerogative with respect to tax legislation is even more sacrosanct than with respect to the power of the purse.

The case may be somewhat different with respect to payroll contributions. They are not regarded as part of the general revenue and are appropriated to special social insurance funds. If the present recommendations for an extended social insurance system are adopted, payroll taxes will increase within a few years to an aggregate of about 10–12%. A variation in this percentage could have a very

---

[22] See "Federal Expenditure and Revenue Policies," Hearings before the Joint Committee on the Economic Report, *op. cit.*, and *National and International Measures for Full Employment, op. cit.*

significant economic effect. There may be fewer objections to an administrative flexibility in social insurance contributions paid into trust accounts than in general taxes. Increases in social insurance contribution schedules by legislation in the past have been repeatedly "frozen" by legislation on short notice, and Congress has recognized that possible future deficits in the funds must be met by appropriations from general Treasury funds. It is perhaps significant that the wartime coalition government in Great Britain also identified social insurance contributions as the most suitable instrument of a flexible tax policy. Still, such variations in social security rates can at best make a moderate contribution to a stabilization policy.

If a delegation of power to vary the rates of either taxes or social insurance contributions, with or without a formula, does not appear acceptable, it is not entirely unrealistic to envisage simplified legislative procedures for enactment of specified changes within a short time. On request of the President, or on its own initiative, the Joint Committee on the Economic Report could, for instance, be authorized to recommend temporary changes in tax rates for purposes of an anticyclical policy. In this case a representative of the Joint Committee might testify before the Ways and Means and Senate Finance Committees and the hearings could be limited to a minimum. The legislation might provide that the changes be for a specified limited period. If changes were intended to become permanent, the limiting clause would have to be eliminated by ordinary legislation, presumably after hearings which would be more detailed and extensive than those held under the simplified procedure.

I believe that neither built-in flexibility, nor formula flexibility, nor delegated flexibility can be the full answer to a cyclical tax policy. To a large extent we must depend on improvements in the normal procedures of tax legislation and on a much closer cooperation of the executive and legislative branches in economic stabilization policy.

6. Conflict in Procedure: Mechanism of Budget Making versus the Need for Flexibility

One specific difficulty with a cyclical consideration of expenditure policy follows not so much from the conflict with legislative control as from the sheer mechanical requirements of budget making. On what assumptions with respect to economic developments should the budget requests of the various agencies be prepared?

With the Call for Estimates, a policy letter formulated by the budget director is sent to the agency telling them by what assumptions they should be guided in preparing their requests for the ensuing year. These assumptions must be formulated more than two years before the end of the period for which the estimates are prepared. The attempt to base the budgetary requirements on anything like a realistic economic forecast seems to be utterly impossible. First, we do not now have, and I doubt that we ever will have, the ability to make a reasonable forecast which covers a period two years hence. . . .

Second, even if forecasts were more reliable than they are it would be difficult to base the budget preparation on them. Budget preparations, for instance, for the fiscal year ending in June, 1955, begin in the spring of 1953. Let us assume, for discussion's sake, that at that time experts expect that business conditions are likely to decline so that at least for part of the fiscal year 1955 depressed conditions should be assumed. Such a "forecast" can only mean that the experts expect a business contraction under the assumption that current government policies continue and that no effective stabilization program of the government is initiated. Under the Employment Act the President would have to make recommendations to Congress to counteract a depression as soon as such a forecast can reliably be made. Assuming the government initiates such counteraction in time, the outlook for the fiscal year 1955 would appear quite different. The downward tendency may be halted or reversed, depending on the promptness and effectiveness of the program. In any case basing the budget preparation on the assumption of a depression in the next fiscal year for purposes of the formulation of departmental requirements would really imply failure on the part of the President or the Congress to take effective measures to forestall or counteract an anticipated depression.

Therefore it appears preferable that the budget as a whole should always be prepared under the assumption of approximately full employment. This budget would show expenditures and revenues, disregarding the effects of a possible business recession. For programs which would be initiated or increased immediately if business should begin to slacken, a contingency appropriation should be requested so that a minor fluctuation does not make it necessary to ask for a deficiency appropriation. This contingency reserve should, however, be impounded, to be released only by specific presidential action. This would make it unnecessary to base the budgetary requirements on any specific forecast, but would make funds available to the President which would be needed in case of a mild depression. In case of a severe depression, however, the President would have to submit to Congress a supplementary or deficiency request for funds for additional programs along with other recommendations for economic and fiscal policies as they would be formulated under the Employment Act.

It is important for Congress and the public to recognize clearly the basis on which budgets are formulated. If a hypothetical full employment basis is used, later revisions may not be due to erroneous estimates but to a discrepancy between assumed and actual events. The budget should be thought of less as a forecast than as a working plan which is designed as the basis for later adaptation to unfolding economic conditions.

7. *Conflict in Accounting*

The conduct of fiscal policy requires estimates of cost for a program as a whole. For deciding whether a program is worth undertaking, and especially for comparing various different accounting guides from those needed for program formulation and program control.

Program formulation requires alternative programs which are under construction, true cost estimates are essential and, as far as possible, appraisals of the benefits to be derived from the program. If, for instance, construction of a dam is under consideration, estimates of the costs and benefits of the whole project are more essential than an estimate of expenditures which would have to be made in the first year.

Program control requires statements which relate the legislative authorization to appropriations, obligations, and actual expenditures. These statements permit a review of the legality of a government activity, of the progress made in its execution, and of the unobligated appropriations and unliquidated obligations (which are factors to be considered in computing the need for new appropriations and for estimating future expenditures).

Financial planning requires estimates of cash expenditures and cash receipts which have an impact on cash balances of the Treasury, and the need to borrow and the possibility of redeeming outstanding indebtedness.

The data developed for program formulation and program control must be adjusted before they can be used as guides for financial planning. While appropriations and obligations for expenditures and tax liabilities are most important for program formulation and program control, financial planning must be based on cash expenditures and cash receipts. Furthermore, accounting according to administrative organizations may very often lead to double counting. Money may be appropriated to trust accounts and reported as budget expenditures or as a reduction from gross receipts.[23] On the other hand, the trust accounts reflect disbursements of these accounts to recipients. The purpose of this administrative accounting is control and supervision. Adding up these administrative accounts does not necessarily give any meaningful totals. Meaningful totals are needed, however, for financial and fiscal planning.

For financial planning, therefore, statements are needed which 1) reflect only cash transactions, 2) include disbursements of all the various government accounts, including accounts of government corporations and trust funds, and 3) eliminate transfers from one government account to another. Such estimates have been called the *consolidated cash statement*. This statement presents meaningful totals.

The consolidated cash statement is not only an instrument for financial planning but also for *fiscal policy*. Fiscal policy views the government budget as an aid in balancing the nation's economic budget. Fiscal policy considerations, therefore, require new concepts and new classifications in government and national economic accounting. Statements are needed for past, current, and future periods that portray the relationship between the government accounts and the national income and expenditure accounts. We must know what money is being spent in a way that adds to the funds available to individuals, businesses, state and local governments, or foreign countries, and what revenue is received through absorption of funds from the same groups.

Traditional budget accounting was developed as a tool for program control, program formulation, financial planning. One cannot say that the budget for the United States has been clearly devised to serve any one of these purposes. It includes cash and noncash transactions, disbursements to the public, and internal transfers.

The various purposes of government accounting should be more clearly distinguished. We need cost data for program appraisal; we need data for purposes of budget control; we need data for financial planning and fiscal policy. No one set of figures can serve all these purposes. The consolidated cash budget and the nation's economic

---

[23] Most receipts from payroll taxes are directly appropriated to the social insurance funds and appear in the budget as a deduction from gross receipts rather than as expenditures.

budget were designed for purposes of financial planning and for guidance of fiscal policy.

Fiscal policy requires not only the development of appropriate totals of budget transactions but also of suitable classifications. With respect to new classifications, the requirements of fiscal policy reinforce the need for a classification by character of expenditure. Such a classification distinguishes between expenditures for current operations and those expenditures which are of an investment nature and hence represent benefits which will be realized in future periods.[24] Furthermore, the fiscal analyst needs expenditures classified according to type of goods and services which are bought (object classification) and also a classification by type of recipients of the money paid out.[25]

The conflict between the conventional accounts and the accounts needed for fiscal policy can be reconciled because the same basic data can be processed in different ways so as to supply various statements, each serving its own purpose.

8. *The Human Conflict*

Perhaps the hardest conflict resides in the fact that the job of conventional budget determination and of fiscal policy requires different attitudes. The people whose job it is to screen budgetary requests and determine either budgetary recommendations or Congressional appropriations must be in a frame of mind which is quite different from that of those who can be most effective in the formulation and determination of fiscal policies. The legislator who has the job of examining budgetary requests usually assumes that the agencies are asking for too much. They know by experience that a good executive who

[24] For an example of such a classification see the *Budget of the United States Government for the Fiscal Year 1952*, pp. 969 ff. For a corresponding discussion related to Great Britain see J. R. Hicks, *The Problem of Budgetary Reform* (Oxford, Clarendon Press, 1948). Hicks deals especially with the problems of accounting for nationalized economic activities in Great Britain. They are of lesser importance in this country, but some corresponding problems exist with respect to, for instance, the Post Office Department, Tennessee Valley Authority, and other agencies with quasi-commercial activities. For a full discussion of the policy use of national economic accounting in various countries, see *Income and Wealth*, Series I, Erik Lundberg, ed., International Association for Research in Income and Wealth (Cambridge, England, Bowes & Bowes, 1951).

[25] As a sample of classification of expenditures by type of recipient, see Table A-8 in the *Midyear Economic Report of the President*, July, 1952, p. 134 f.

is devoted to his task wants to do the best possible job, and the best possible job requires money. He wants efficiency, too, but he usually wants efficiency not in order to reduce the amount of money needed but to do a better job with the same amount.

Thus the legislator feels called upon to counteract this natural drive toward expansion. Of course there is also the tendency that legislators want more money appropriated for purposes in which their constituents are particularly interested. But the expenditures in which a legislator has a particular interest need not be the same as those for which the executive is making his request.

The same is largely true with respect to an efficient screening of budgetary requests on the executive side. True, the Budget Bureau is an important management arm of the President and wants to see that the President's program is implemented by budgetary allowances. The late Budget Director, Harold D. Smith, often emphasized that he no longer regarded it as the main function of the budget director to act as the "watchdog of the Treasury," but that he felt the budget director is responsible for implementing the President's program in the most efficient and economical manner. Nevertheless, a comparison between agency requests and final budget recommendations shows that the Budget Bureau has continued to perform its watchdog functions effectively. Budget examiners by the very nature of their job must adopt a critical attitude toward budgetary requests and often regard the amount of dollars they are able to cut from a departmental request as a measurement of their effectiveness. There is certainly an urgent need for an effective performance of this screening job.

As long as the economy is in a state of inflationary pressures, the attitude of legislative or executive budget examiners coincides largely with the requirements of a restraining fiscal policy. In a period of threatening or actual business contraction, however, fiscal policy may require the stepping-up of government activities rather than curtailment. There is certainly the danger that in such a period the fiscal policy view and the budget view may clash. To some extent such a clash did occur at the beginning of the thirties when Budget Director Douglas showed little enthusiasm in implementing the President's recovery program.

As a matter of fact, it would be utterly erroneous to have a looser attitude toward budget requirements in a period of under-employment than in a period of high employment. We need stabilization policies but the attitude toward budgetary screening should always be strict and conscientious. In the postwar years the Budget

Bureau's policy letter accompanying the Call for Estimates has emphasized the need for tight budgeting in an inflationary period. It cannot be imagined that the Budget Bureau would or should ever send out a policy letter that did not ask for tight budgeting. Programs should always be executed with a minimum amount of money. What should be changed is the size and character of the *programs* rather than the attitude toward economy in budgeting.

The President's program should be determined after consideration primarily of long-range and secondarily of short-range economic and noneconomic objectives and the total costs involved. The budgetary review should insure that these programs are formulated and executed with the greatest economy at all times. The Executive Office of the President must assist the President in both these functions, namely, the formulation of a program that takes account of economic requirements and also the most economical implementation of his program. The Executive Office needs two types of people: those who have the attitude and imagination to be able to assist the President in program formulation and those who have the attitude and conscientiousness of the budget examiner.[26]

Whatever the best administrative relationship may be between these two groups within the Executive Office, it is clear that both attitudes must be blended if a national program is to be formulated that fulfills the necessary functions of supporting an expanding economy, assure that waste is eliminated, and that the nation receives the highest possible value from each dollar spent.

[26] Thomas Blaisdell, Jr., probably had the distinction between these two attitudes in mind when, in a speech before the American Society for Public Administration in Washington, D. C., March 11, 1949, he said: "The Budget Bureau methods are those of the control of the purse strings. The methods of the Council of Economic Advisers must be those of leading strings."

PART THREE

RELIANCE ON AUTOMATIC BUDGET STABILIZERS: TWO OPPOSING VIEWS

Committee for Economic Development

Taxes and the Budget: A Program for Prosperity in a Free Economy*

The stabilizing budget policy recommended by the Committee for Economic Development relies on a system of built-in flexibility and automatic stabilizers rather than the discretionary policy favored in varying degree by the two preceding authors, Lerner and Colm. In this approach, the government should set tax rates to achieve a budget balance or small surplus at a specific level of income and employment, yield increasing surpluses if this level of income is exceeded and growing deficits if it falls increasingly short of the mark. These surpluses and deficits would occur automatically through

* Reprinted by permission from *Taxes and the Budget: A Program for Prosperity in a Free Economy* (Committee for Economic Development, Part I, New York, November 1947).

the functioning of the tax and expenditure system. As income fell below the prescribed level, deficits would result as tax revenues declined and certain expenditures, such as unemployment compensation, rose. These changes would reduce the severity of any economic contraction and help set the stage for recovery. If income rose to an inflationary level, above what was considered a normal full employment one, surpluses would develop due to automatic increases in tax revenues and decreases in outlays. This would help stem any tendency toward continued inflation. In the view of its sponsors, this fiscal program, together with other tools, notably flexible monetary policy, would keep economic instability within tolerable limits. To try to accomplish more, it is felt, would be futile because of our limited predictive ability. The government, if it were to rush in with frequent changes in expenditures and tax rates, would contribute to uncertainty and, therefore, might well aggravate instability. Also, it would more likely intervene to fight unemployment than inflation; this would contribute toward long-run inflation and probably to an increasing level of government expenditures, both of which results are viewed with concern by the C.E.D. Under its program, any increase in government spending would be financed by higher taxes, preserving the principle of budget balance at a given income level. This would serve to keep the principle of weighing costs against benefits in the forefront and thus contribute to fiscal responsibility, by which is usually meant a rein on expenditures. In case of severe inflation or depression, the C.E.D. would accept departure from its program and allow some discretionary action.

"WHAT will this mean to me?" is the first question that the average man asks when he thinks of taxes or government expenditures. It is natural for us as individuals to consider federal government finance as it affects us directly in terms of the taxes we ourselves pay, the government services we ourselves enjoy, and the government bonds we ourselves own. But the real importance of government finance lies not in these things. It lies in the consequences for all of us of the taxes *everyone* pays, and in the effect upon us of the *total* government debt and the *total* government expenditures.

Government financial policy benefits or hurts us all by the way in which it helps to answer the following questions:

What are our prospects for steady employment and income?

What are the risks that inflation will reduce the buying power of our income and our savings?

Will we have the opportunity to enjoy during our lifetime a continuing improvement of our standard of living such as our parents and grandparents knew in theirs?

Will we and our children have the opportunity for continued enjoyment of the blessings of a free society?

These are vital questions. They constitute the fundamental tests by which government financial policy and action must be judged. This policy statement explains the connection between government finance and economic progress, freedom and stability and presents a program to serve these objectives. The program consists of two related parts: a) budgetary policy to set the proper relation between government expenditures and government receipts, and b) tax policy to raise the necessary revenues in the ways most appropriate to the objectives. Economic stability and progress in a free society require sound public policy not only in taxation and the budget but also in other areas — including money and credit, management of the debt and labor-management relations. These subjects and others are now being studied under the CED Research Program. The recommendations of this policy statement are offered as part of a rounded program of government and private action which must be developed for a solution of our basic economic problems.

GOVERNMENT FINANCIAL POLICY, HIGH EMPLOYMENT AND STABLE PRICES

The level of employment and prices is governed largely by the total demand for goods and services. Total demand is the combined amount that individuals, businesses, governments and foreign purchasers are willing and able to buy. Both "willingness" and "ability" are essential. No amount of money or credit or income would be large enough to assure adequate demand if individuals and businesses were not willing to use it for consumption or investment. There must be ability to buy — but ability to buy does not alone create demand.

When total demand exceeds the output that can be produced with the available materials, labor and equipment — as it has since the start of the war — prices rise, and we suffer the now-familiar evils of inflation. When total demand is inadequate to buy the output that would be produced by a fully employed labor force — as it was in the 30's — we have depression, unemployment and falling prices. *An essential condition for high employment and stable prices is reasonable stability of total demand at an adequate level — which means a steadily rising level of demand as our productive capacity grows.*

The level of total demand is the composite product of millions of individual decisions to spend or invest which are made by consumers, businesses and governments. The federal government cannot possibly control these decisions, and a system in which the government tried to exercise such control would be intolerable to freedom-loving people. But the government cannot help influencing these decisions that affect total demand through its taxes, expenditures and borrowing — its fiscal policy.

A major factor in the decisions of individuals and businesses to spend or invest is the amount of income they have available. In collecting taxes the government subtracts from the available income of individuals and businesses. On the other hand, federal expenditures add to the incomes available for private expenditure. By its policy with respect to the amount and timing of these subtractions from and additions to private income, the government inevitably influences the separate decisions of millions of individuals.

Many of the decisions that enter into total demand are based not so much upon current available income as upon the prospect for future earnings. This is particularly true of business decisions to invest — to launch new products, to build new plants, to buy new machinery. The question here is whether the investment seems likely to yield to the investor a return sufficient to compensate for the risks and costs involved. In these decisions federal tax policy — especially through the rates and character of taxes on profits — bears a heavy weight.

The size of the public debt, its form, and who holds it also are important factors affecting individual and business expenditure. For instance, if the government sells savings bonds to the public, and uses the proceeds to retire bonds held by the banks, individuals will have less cash and are likely to buy less.

In addition to influencing private demand in these various ways, the government directly controls another large part of total demand — its own demand for goods and services. The federal government is by far the largest single employer of labor and purchaser of supplies. Although government expenditure should decline, it will remain large enough to have a great influence upon the adequacy of total demand.

Fiscal policy is not a panacea for all the problems of maintaining high employment and price stability. Even perfect stability of total demand, if it could be achieved, would not eliminate all fluctuations in employment or the general level of prices. Nor can fiscal action by itself achieve complete stability of total demand. Since we are dealing with the independent decisions of millions of separate units — in a free economy this will always be true — fiscal policy cannot completely iron out fluctuations in total demand. The picture of an all-wise expert precisely manipulating the keys of the fiscal instrument to produce a perfect harmony of stable demand is sheer, and dangerous, fantasy. But if we manage our fiscal affairs as well as we know how, duly recognizing their impact on employment and prices, we shall be contributing much more than ever before to a continuing high level of economic activity. And if we supplement this with intelligent behavior in other fields, such as money, banking and foreign trade, we may reasonably expect to maintain a high level of productive employment.

FISCAL POLICY AND ECONOMIC PROGRESS

During the past century, the real output produced by an hour's work in the United States has approximately doubled in each generation. This rapid — unparalleled — growth of productivity has been a major source of America's strength. It has meant more than a continuous improvement of the material welfare of the American people. Every sector of the population has been able to look forward to further improvement simultaneously with other sectors, and not at the expense of other groups; economic progress has been important in reducing potential friction among groups. Moreover, America's lead in productivity on two occasions has enabled a non-militarist democracy to overcome the armed challenge of militarist dictatorships.

Two essentials for economic progress are: a) *the willingness of individuals to devote effort, imagination and capital to increased production, more efficient production and the production of new things, and b) the supply of capital ready to move into the frontiers of economic development.* In the United States both of these factors have been abundant. The American system has held forth the chances of large rewards to persons who would turn their efforts or funds to economic development. This *chance* for large rewards was the driving force behind countless ventures. Many of them failed but large numbers succeeded, in smaller or greater measure, and pushed upward the curve of economic progress. The profits from the successful enterprises constituted a large flow of capital into the hands of venturesome, energetic, imaginative persons willing to risk this capital in further development. The point is not merely that we had a large supply of savings; the savings were attracted to participate in the *risks* of economic enterprise.

Today our economy faces a new situation. Except in war or its aftermath, we have never endured taxes as high as we now face. This means that federal taxes will be taking a much larger proportion than ever before of the income that must provide the incentives to individual enterprise and the sources of private capital investment. We cannot hope to return in the near future to tax levels as low as those before the war. But we must do our utmost to reduce taxes by economy in government expenditure, and we must distribute the remaining burden in the ways least damaging to progress.

FISCAL POLICY AND FREEDOM

Fiscal policy, because of its effects upon employment, prices and progress, has a direct relation to the preservation of our freedoms. There is danger that if we fail to achieve the goals of stability and progress by methods appropriate to a free society the public may turn to measures of control inimical to freedom without realizing their consequences. It is not only our own freedoms that are at stake. The world looks to the United States for a demonstration of the ability of a free society to solve its basic economic problems.

There is another vital way in which fiscal policy affects the survival of a free society. A free society must have a competitive, decentralized economy. In such an economy the power of any individual to make decisions affecting the welfare of others — decisions as to prices, wages and output — is limited by the existence of actual or potential competitors in the market.

Essential to a competitive economy is "A climate in which new, small and independent business can be conceived and born, can grow and prosper. . . If the opportunities for new business are destroyed or otherwise disappear, a system of free enterprise will atrophy."[1]

A tax system that discourages new and independent business and arrests the growth of established businesses therefore is a threat to a free economy and a free society. The present tax system does

[1] "The Economics of a Free Society," CED Supplementary Paper, by William Benton, *Fortune,* October, 1944.

this. It bears most heavily upon those characteristics most likely to be associated with newness, independence, growth and competitive vigor in business. It erects a barrier to the success of businesses that are especially risky, that have widely fluctuating earnings, or that are highly dependent upon internal financing. By creating a tax system that will be fair to all businesses we can contribute greatly to the vitality of our free society.

Budgetary Policy

. . . In the present section we shall consider the requisites of a budgetary policy — a policy with respect to the relation between total government revenues and total expenditures — to achieve the basic objectives we have outlined.

THE PRINCIPLES OF BUDGETARY POLICY

Four considerations are of supreme importance in the development of budgetary policy:

a) *Federal finance should help to make fluctuations in total demand less severe, and thus aid in stabilizing employment and prices.* When total demand exceeds total supply and inflationary conditions prevail, the effect of federal finance should be to restrain demand. When total demand is low, when unemployment is high and prices falling, the effect of taxation and expenditure should be to stimulate demand.

b) *Budgetary policy should serve to restrain unnecessary government expenditure and to stimulate efficiency in government.* Everyone agrees that economy in government is important. But the *achievement of economy* requires that our *belief in economy* be effectively directed against the particular pressures that always will be found in support of particular expenditures. Budgetary policy can be an effective force for economy if we harness the legitimate and specific interest in lower taxes to the general interest in economy. Every proposal that would expand government functions should pass the test of society's willingness to pay for it in taxes.

c) *Budgetary policy should provide for the reduction of the public debt under conditions of reasonably high employment and production.* The interest charge on the debt now accounts for about ten per cent of our federal tax load. Surely we cannot think that these taxes are burdenless because we pay the proceeds to ourselves in interest. The deterrent effects of high taxes upon risk-taking and incentives to effort are not at all offset by the payment of interest on government debt; interest on the government debt is not the kind of income that is most important to reward or stimulate private effort or enterprise.

d) *Budgetary policy should recognize that it takes a long time to make most fiscal decisions and achieve their effects, and that the present state of our ability to forecast economic fluctuations is still very low.* Any fiscal program that relies for its success upon prompt response and adjustment to known economic changes through a series of separate decisions, or upon accurate forecasting of future fluctuations, invites failure.

There are some particular measures that can be initiated so quickly and, if necessary, reversed so promptly that they involve only short and relatively safe forecasts. But success in the year-to-year operation of most elements of fiscal policy requires that minimum reliance be placed upon forecasting economic fluctuations.

WHAT'S IN THE BUDGET?

Before we can decide on budgetary policy, it is necessary to make clear what we mean by "the budget."

There are two "budgets" of the federal government officially compiled and in current use. These are the administrative budget and the consolidated-cash budget. The administrative budget does what the budget system was first created to do — to enable the Congress and the President to control the expenditures and operations of the hundreds of agencies that constitute the federal government. It does this by stating in detail the funds appropriated to each agency and purpose, the obligations incurred for expenditure under each of these heads, and the amounts spent out of each fund, including amounts paid or transferred to other accounts. Beyond this administrative function, this budget, together with its supplementary statements, serves another purpose. It presents an accounting statement of the financial relations of the various federal agencies, corporations and trust accounts to the public and to each other.

The other budget — the consolidated-cash budget — is designed for quite a different purpose. It shows the government's financial transactions as they affect the whole economy — the expenditures that absorb goods and services or add to private incomes, the receipts that subtract from private incomes, the deficits or surpluses that add to or subtract from the public's holdings of money and government bonds.

The dollars that affect demand are the dollars paid to or taken from the public, not the dollars transferred from one government account to another. Therefore, in the consolidated-cash budget all transactions between one part of the government and another are excluded. And since the transactions that are significant for total demand are those that involve receipt or payment of money, this budget is on a "cash" basis. All cash transactions between the government — and this includes all government agencies, corporations, and trust accounts — and the public are shown. It excludes all transactions not involving payment of money to the public or receipt of money from the public.

The recommendations of this policy statement are framed throughout with reference to the consolidated-cash budget.

In recent budget messages of the President a statement of the federal accounts on a consolidated-cash basis has been utilized as supplementary information to make clear the relationship of federal financial operations to the economy. The consolidated-cash budget has also been used in the President's Economic Reports as the significant representation of the economic effects of federal finance. In its policy statement, "Fiscal Policy to Fight Inflation" (September, 1946), the Research and Policy Committee of CED based its quantitative recommendations on this budget. Other business organizations and non-governmental groups concerned with the impact of federal finance upon the economy have turned increasingly to the picture shown by the consolidated-cash budget. A few illustrations will show the nature of the distinction between the two budgets.

Because the consolidated-cash budget excludes all intra-government transactions, it does not show as an expenditure the transfers from the general government accounts to, for example, the trust accounts set up for the operation of the social security system. Such transactions are important to the administrative budget for recording the status of the various accounts in relation to each other. But the transfers are not transactions with important current economic effects.

At the same time, there are billions of dollars of receipts and expenditures that appear in the consolidated-cash budget but are not included in the administrative budget. The outstanding case is the payroll tax receipts and expenditures of the social security system. Present legal and accounting relations between the general government and the trust accounts are best revealed if these transactions are shown separately from other receipts and expenditures. But if we want to weigh the effects of the budget upon private purchasing power, total demand, employment and prices, the budget must include these important collections and payments.

The "cash" character of the consolidated-cash budget is illustrated by the treatment of the issue and redemption of veterans' terminal leave bonds. For fiscal 1947 the administrative budget included as an expenditure about $2 billion to reflect the issue of these non-negotiable non-cashable bonds in that year. Their economic effect was small; in fact, terminal leave was paid in this form to prevent the payment from having inflationary consequences. The consolidated-cash budget did not include this item as an expenditure. In fiscal 1948, when about $1.5 billion of these bonds are being turned into cash, much of which will be used for consumption, the administrative budget shows no expenditure in this account. But the fiscal 1948 consolidated-cash budget does include this $1.5 billion payment because it is now actually being put into the hands of individuals as expendable income.[2]

The size of the net difference between the two budgets varies from year to year. Thus, in fiscal 1947, the surplus in the consolidated-cash budget was almost $6 billion larger than the surplus in the administrative budget. But, by contrast, official estimates are that the consolidated-cash surplus in fiscal 1948 will be $5.5 billion and the administrative surplus $4.7 billion — a difference of $800 million. (The indicated surplus for calendar 1948 is much larger.) Under some conditions the consolidated-cash surplus would be smaller than the administrative surplus. Many of the differences between the two budgets relate to the time at which various transactions are recorded; over a reasonably long period — say ten years — these differences would cancel out. At present, the most important *persistent* difference between the two budgets is in the treatment of the social security trust accounts. Over a ten year period, the consolidated-cash surplus would exceed the administrative surplus by approximately the amount of surplus in the social security accounts. If the social security system were set up so that its expenditures and receipts balanced over a moderate period, the average surplus in the consolidated-cash budget would be roughly the same as the average surplus in the administrative budget.[3]

2 Similarly, the consolidated-cash budget shows interest on savings bonds as an expenditure when it is paid in cash, while the administrative budget includes the interest as it accrues. In both budgets taxes are included in receipts when collected, not when the liability accrues.

3 The consolidated-cash budget bears no relation to the "dual budget" or "capital budget" system sometimes proposed during the depression. These budgets called for division of government expenditures into two categories, one to include all expenditures that resulted in "capital assets," such as public

THE THREE ALTERNATIVES IN BUDGET POLICY

There are three distinct alternatives in budgetary policy:

1. *The annually-balanced budget policy.* This policy attempts to keep government revenues continuously equal to or in excess of government expenditures, regardless of economic conditions.

2. *The managed compensatory budget policy.* Under this policy, attempts would be made to adjust tax rates and expenditure programs as often as necessary and to the extent necessary to keep employment or the national income steady at a high level.

3. *The stabilizing budget policy.* This policy is described herein, and advocated as the most practical method of achieving all the objectives of budgetary policy. Its basic principle is to set tax rates to balance the budget and provide a surplus at agreed high levels of employment and national income and thereafter to leave them alone unless there is some major change in national policy or condition of national life.

ANNUAL BUDGET BALANCING

The annual-balance policy cannot be made to work, and the effort to make it work accentuates inflations and depressions. With its inevitable breakdown fiscal policy becomes a mere day-to-day expedient.

This program requires that, whenever a decrease in the national income is forecast, tax rates must be raised or expenditures cut, or both, to prevent a budget deficit. Whenever the forecast of higher national income promises larger surpluses, it not only permits but invites a cut in tax rates and a rise in expenditure programs. On the record, the program meant tax cuts in the prosperous 20's, and tax increases in the depressed 30's.

The implications of such a program are clear:

a) Tax rates and expenditure programs will be changed at times and in directions most harmful to high employment and stable prices. When incomes are low and unemployment is widespread, tax rates must be raised and government expenditures cut. In boom times the program welcomes tax reductions and new expenditures.

b) Annual budget-balancing policy does not in the long run pro-

buildings or dams. This system moved in exactly the opposite direction from the consolidated-cash budget, which seeks to present a unified picture of the transactions that have important economic effects, without regard to financial or functional differences.

mote government economy. The program allows a growth of public expenditure in boom times, without any increase of tax rates, even with a decrease in tax rates. The policy does not furnish steady pressure against the initiation of unnecessary expenditures; the pressure it does provide, to end entrenched expenditure programs in depressions, is certain to be ineffective.

c) The system dissipates the potentially large surpluses of good times and strives vainly for balance in bad times. In a fluctuating economy this program will not result in debt reduction.

d) To carry out the program requires a degree of accuracy in forecasting fluctuations in business activity that has not been achieved in the past and that is not possible now.

e) The program involves irregular and unpredictable variations of tax rates, with unsettling effects upon business and personal planning.

THE MANAGED COMPENSATORY BUDGET POLICY

The theory of the managed compensatory budget is simple. Whenever employment is judged "about to be" below a high level, taxes should be cut and expenditures increased by the amount necessary to prevent the forecast from coming true. Whenever prices seem "about to be" above the proper level, tax rates must be raised and expenditures cut.

Dependence upon accurate forecasting of business fluctuations is even greater for the compensatory budget than for the annually-balanced budget. If forecasting is inaccurate, the compensatory budget could easily increase fluctuations rather than moderate them.

Like the annually balanced budget system, the compensatory program encourages increased expenditure programs without higher tax rates at some stage of the business cycle. However, whereas the annually balanced budget plan opens the door to new spending in boom times, the compensatory plan opens the door in depression — actual or forecast. In either case the effect upon government economy is likely to be the same — periods of rapid increases in spending, followed by futile efforts at retrenchment and a generally excessive upward drift of expenditures.

If the managed compensatory system is to make any progress towards reducing the debt, it must count upon creating large surpluses in prosperous periods by raising taxes and cutting expenditures. But expenditures resist downward change and taxes resist upward change. In the present state of economic forecasting, it will always be possible to make out a plausible case that depression is around the corner. Such a prediction will permit both unpleasant alternatives to be avoided, since under the managed compensatory theory the forecast of depression requires lower tax rates and higher expenditures. This system offers no realistic hope of debt reduction.

Under this plan, as under the annual-balance plan, tax rates are subject to frequent and unsettling changes.

THE STABILIZING BUDGET POLICY: WHAT IT IS

The key to a program that will promote stability, government economy and debt reduction without requiring impossible accuracy of forecasting business fluctuations is this:

Set tax rates to balance the budget and provide a surplus for debt retirement at an agreed high level of employment and national income. Having set these rates, leave them alone unless there is some major change in national policy or condition of national life.

Tax *rates,* by themselves, do not determine how much revenue will be collected. The *rates* merely say, for example, that revenue will be $9 per gallon of liquor sold, $38 per $100 of corporate profits, $50 per $100 of individual taxable income within a certain bracket, and so on. How much will be collected with these rates depends upon the amount of liquor sold, the amount of corporate profits, and the amount of individual incomes. Since all of the important elements of the tax base are closely related to the national income, collections under any system of unchanging tax rates will be larger as the national income rises and smaller as the national income falls.

Some kinds of government expenditures also tend to vary automatically with economic conditions. Unemployment compensation payments are the outstanding case. When unemployment rises these payments also rise, and when unemployment drops the payments decline. In addition, some expenditures — such as public works — may be advanced or held back to meet changing economic conditions within the limits of an agreed total expenditure program.

With tax rates set to yield a moderate surplus at high-employment national income, larger surpluses will result when the national income is above that level. At lower national incomes the surplus will be smaller and below some point there will be deficits.

Under this system, surpluses arising when national income goes above the standard high-employment level should not be used to increase expenditures. Likewise, a reduction of tax rates without a corresponding reduction of expenditures would be contrary to the policy, regardless of the *actual* surplus at the *actual* national income (subject to exceptions that will be stated below).

A direct consequence of the stabilizing budget principle is that fluctuations in the national income do not call for fluctuations in tax rates, or in expenditures except for the automatic response of some expenditure items. However, changes in tax rates or expenditures will be appropriate under some circumstances. If, for example, improvement of the international situation should lead to a substantial reduction in annual expenditure for defense, a lowering of tax rates would be appropriate. Similarly, if a new program is to be adopted that will substantially raise the annual level of federal spending, higher tax rates will be required.

Three exceptions should be noted to the general principle that tax *rates* and expenditures should only change up or down in step with each other:

1) With a growing population and rising productivity, the national income at high employment will gradually rise. Therefore, the yield of a constant system of tax rates at the standard high-employment national income will also slowly and steadily increase. This gradual increase of tax yield will permit, without higher tax rates, some gradual increase in normal government expenditure that may accompany the growth of the population and the national income. Moreover, as the economy grows into higher income levels, the amount of debt reduction consistent with high employment and stable prices may increase also; if so, the increased yield of the tax system should be retained for that purpose. Any readjustment of tax rates made possible by the long-time growth of the tax base should be made at reasonable intervals, say five years, in order to avoid the unsettling effects of annual rate changes.

2) From time to time an urgent need may arise for an extraordinary expenditure that is large in amount but known to be temporary. It would probably be undesirable to raise tax rates sharply in order to finance such expenditures currently, and then to cut tax rates when the expenditure ceases. A plan for meeting these expenditures over a somewhat longer period would therefore be appropriate. This plan might take the form of a smaller tax rate increase, extended over a longer period. If the expenditure is in the form of loans, the repayments may provide the source from which the expenditure will, in the end, be met. Whatever the plan for ultimately financing the expenditure, any immediate inflationary consequences of the expenditure should be offset by anti-inflationary borrowing. Outlays under a program for foreign rehabilitation may fall within this exception.

3) The recommendations of this report are presented in the belief that, if they are combined with appropriate measures in other fields, economic fluctuations can be confined to moderate departures from a high level. Yet it would be foolhardy to ignore the possibility that we may again confront an economic crisis of great magnitude — either severe depression or major inflation. Some extraordinary action must and will be taken if such a crisis appears. An emergency Congressional reduction or increase in tax rates (perhaps with a fixed, automatic termination date) would then be one of the most effective and least dangerous of the available courses.

How the Stabilizing Budget Policy Works

The policy recommended here cannot be "adopted" and left to run without common sense and vigilance. Basically, we are presenting the principles that are important in making the decisions that must be made. The policy will not yield the results of which it is capable unless the principles are consistently followed and reasonably interpreted.

Any policy faces the danger that those responsible for administering it will not accept it or, giving lip-service to it, will seek to evade its intent. This is not a peculiarity of the policy recommended here. The first essential for the success of any policy is the existence of a *will* to carry it out. But it would be undue cynicism, unjustified by experience, to believe that reasonable adherence to principles is unattainable.

The policy of the stabilizing budget is more likely to be consistently followed than either of the alternative policies, simply because it is easier. It does not call for unachievable accuracy in forecasting economic fluctuations or impossible speed in action. It does not seek to impose an intolerable and unattainable increase of tax rates in the face of unemployment and shrinking income.

The enactment of the Legislative Reorganization Act in 1946 provides basis for confidence in the development of a determination by the government to carry out a policy such as is recommended here. The most important feature of the Act, from the standpoint of this program, is that it recognizes the need for a Congressional fiscal program as distinguished from a series of unrelated fiscal actions. This Act and the Employment Act of 1946 gave us for the first time Congressional mechanisms that begin to approach adequacy for formulating and executing a Congressional budget. These mechanisms need to be strengthened and improved. Particularly, responsibility needs to be centered upon the majority party to adopt a legislative budget and to follow it in appropriations and tax legislation. But at least a start has been made toward the development of new Congressional machinery that can make possible an integrated Congressional fiscal policy.

At present, the President submits to the Congress each year a budget of estimated receipts and disbursements under existing and proposed expenditure authorizations and tax laws. The four revenue and appropriations committees of the two Houses of Congress, acting jointly, then prepare a legislative budget. The committees present their recommended budget, including estimates of total receipts and expenditures, to the two Houses for adoption. When adopted, this budget serves as a guide to Congressional action on appropriations and taxes.

Aside from the improvements of this procedure that are needed to make *any* fiscal policy work, the stabilizing budget policy involves three changes from present practice:

1) The budget used by the President and the Congress in decisions on total receipts and expenditures should be the consolidated-cash budget, rather than the administrative budget.

2) Estimates of revenue yield from existing or recommended taxes should be based on a high-employment national income, rather than upon a forecast of arbitrarily selected national income.

3) The program recommended here suggests a standard to be followed by the President and the Congress in deciding upon the relation between total receipts and total expenditures. That standard is that the consolidated-cash budget should show a moderate surplus at an agreed high-employment level of national income. There does not now seem to be any standard generally accepted or consistently applied.

How the Stabilizing Budget Policy Promotes Economic Stability

The automatic change in tax collections and government outlays with fluctuations in the national income is an essential feature of the program recommended here. This kind of variation is precisely what is required if fiscal policy is to aid economic stability. When employment, production and prices rise, national income will rise. As the national income rises, tax collections will rise, taking more and more from the available income of the public. At the same time, outlays under such programs as unemployment compensation will fall. This process will restrain increases of demand and curb inflationary pressure. Similarly, the automatic decline of tax revenue acts to check a downward movement. When production and income drop, tax collections will fall too. Income after taxes will decline less than income before taxes. This will help to sustain production and employment. The stabilizing effect will be reinforced by an increase in unemployment compensation and other payments.

In other words, *with stable tax rates* variations in tax yields and outlays will tend to cushion variations in available incomes, after tax, and thereby to lessen fluctuations in demand and production. This is not new, but its importance has grown greatly since before the war for the following reasons:

1) Even with strenuous efforts for economy, federal taxes for some time will be much higher in relation to the national income than they were before the war.

2) Greater reliance upon the progressive income tax means greater relative change in tax collections with any change in national income. When a wage-earner goes on part-time work, for example, his consumption of tobacco, gasoline, and other commodities subject to excise taxation is unlikely to fall to zero, or even to fall in proportion to his loss of income. But his income tax is very likely to fall to zero and will certainly fall relatively more than his income.

3) The pay-as-you-go, withholding method of income tax payments has greatly shortened the time between a drop in an individual's income and the consequent reduction in his income tax payments. For most taxpayers, changes in income and changes in tax are simultaneous.

4) Unemployment compensation is new and has only recently begun to approach its potentialities as a stabilizing force. Unemployment compensation benefits under present laws would increase about $175 million per year for every million increase in unemployment, and this amount would be higher if desirable extensions of coverage and improvements of benefits were made.

These developments have given us an instrument, which, *if we allow it to operate,* will be a new, powerful force for economic stability.

The great advantage of the automatic corrective response of tax revenues and expenditures is this: *It does not depend for its stabilizing effect upon an impossible accuracy in forecasting economic fluctuations or an impossible speed in making fiscal decisions and taking fiscal action.*

Public Works and Conservation

It is probably now generally agreed that what can be done toward stabilizing the economy by varying the timing of public construction and conservation expenditures is fairly small, in relation to the total problem. But once its limitations are recognized, the programming of public works and conservation projects can make a valuable contribution. Both money and resources will be economized if the government, or any other public or private body with stable prospects, concentrates its building in periods when total construction activity is low. At the same time, this will make for the stability of the construction industry and indirectly of the whole economy.

Success in such a program will depend upon the quality of advance preparations. As far as possible, financial, engineering and administrative arrangements should be completed on a reserve of diverse projects to be started quickly when necessary. The scope of useful action will be expanded by coordination of federal plans with those of state and local governments.

There are two clear dangers in a federal program of this sort. First, attempts to apply the principle to projects involving a long construction period may result in federal construction in fact reaching its peak when other construction activity is high. Second, the countercyclical program can be made the excuse for commitments to continuing programs of a character, location and volume that are inappropriate for the federal government. These dangers can be avoided in a program of modest size, but their avoidance will require constant attention, both by the executive departments and the Congress.

How the Stabilizing Budget Policy Promotes Economy

No budget rule can be a substitute for a real interest in government economy and efficiency. But if interest in economy exists, adherence to sound fiscal principles can help restrain unnecessary expenditure. Under the program recommended here, a proposed increase of expenditures will require raising tax rates.[4] The social costs of particular undertakings will become sharply visible in the form of higher tax rates. It may then be possible to bring these costs properly into balance with the social gains of expenditure when decisions are made.

With the stabilizing budget policy, the close link between expenditures and tax *rates* will be kept at all stages of the business cycle. A high national income and an extraordinary surplus will not mean that additional expenditures should be assumed without an increase of tax rates. Nor will the fact that unemployment exists or is

---

[4] Certain exceptions to this principle have been noted a) to the extent of the growth of tax yields with the rise of population and productivity, b) for large temporary disbursements and c) for advancing the execution of public works and conservation in a time of depressed total construction activity.

forecast justify the addition of new federal expenditures without higher tax rates, except perhaps in extreme circumstances.

The surest road to economy is to prevent the initiation of unnecessary expenditure programs. *No policy that invites or permits new expenditures at any stage of the business cycle merely because they appear painless to the taxpayer can hope in the long run to result in government economy. The really frightening possibility is that we shall oscillate between adherence to the annual balance principle in prosperity and belief in compensatory spending in depression. This could only mean an endless ascent to higher and higher government spending, both in prosperity and depression.*

How the Stabilizing Budget Policy Promotes Debt Reduction

Will adherence to the stabilizing budget policy in fact result in reduction of the debt over a reasonable period of time? The answer to this question depends upon two factors: the standard level of income at which the budget is set to yield a surplus, and the level of income that actually prevails. If the actual income level on the average exceeds the level at which the yield of the tax system equals the expenditures, the debt will be reduced. If on the average the national income falls short of this level, the debt will be increased. Budgetary policy alone — the determination of tax rates and expenditure programs — cannot assure debt reduction. It can only establish the conditions under which the debt would be reduced.

Tax rates could be set high enough to yield a surplus even at a very low level of national income. If this were done, the debt might be reduced despite the prevalence of large-scale unemployment. But, in this case, the budget would exert a repressive force upon the economy in depressed conditions, as it did in the 30's, and would itself contribute to unemployment and a low level of income. While such a program is conceivable, it is certainly not a satisfactory solution to the problem of the debt, and it is unlikely that such a program could survive the pressures that mass unemployment would create, as past experience has shown.

The policy recommended here is to set tax rates high enough to yield a moderate surplus at a high level of employment, and to utilize fully all appropriate means to assure that high employment is maintained. Such a program recognizes the interdependence of all aspects of economic policy.

A sound structure of taxes would be a major contribution to debt reduction under the program laid down here. Collecting the needed revenues in the ways that are least restrictive of private demand for goods and services will assist in the maintenance of high employment along with debt reduction. Other measures that would have similar effects include action in the field of money and banking, the management of the debt, farsighted policy by business and labor in their attitude towards technical progress and productivity, arrangements to improve the flow of savings into constructive investment, and many other instruments. These subjects are under study by the CED as part of its research program on high employment. From the work already done, we are confident that — with reasonably good sense — levels of employment can be maintained that will reduce the debt under this program.

The Committee recommends that tax rates be set sufficiently high to yield a surplus of about $3 billion at a national income corresponding to employment of about 96 per cent of the labor force. With a labor force of the present size, this would mean a $3 billion surplus if unemployment is about 2.5 million. The budget would balance when unemployment is approximately 4 to 4.5 million.

These precise figures cannot be rigorously defended against other figures in the same neighborhood and some adjustments may be indicated after the system has been in operation. However, the appropriate figures cannot be far away in either direction. Actual unemployment may, from time to time, lie below 4 per cent, as it does now; it probably cannot be much below this figure without serious inflationary pressure. With 4 per cent unemployment, most involuntary idleness is of the between-jobs variety. To set tax rates so that the budget yields a moderate surplus only at a higher income level would therefore mean that debt would be reduced only under conditions which it should be public policy to avoid. On the other hand, tax rates high enough to reduce debt at a much lower income level would put deflationary pressure on the economy, and promote unemployment.

THE MANAGEMENT OF THE DEBT

The Committee intends to issue a separate policy statement discussing the management of the debt. Here we wish to emphasize only that the success of the budget policy we are recommending will be strongly influenced by the effectiveness of debt management.

Most people regard the federal debt as a single undifferentiated total. They think of debt policy as simply using the surplus to pay the debt.

There are in fact many different kinds of federal debt — some held by the public and some held by banks, some long-term and some short-term, some marketable and some not. These different kinds of debt differ in their economic effects — such as their effects on inflation and deflation. With the debt at its present size the differentiations are extremely important.

The problem of debt management is to choose the kinds of debt to retire when there is a surplus, and the kind of debt to issue when there is a deficit or when outstanding debt matures. These choices must be made with an understanding of their economic effects if we are to have both high employment and continuous debt reduction.

WHAT PRICE LEVEL?

Selection of the standard national income at which a surplus of a specified size is to be developed requires the selection of a price level, just as it requires the selection of an employment level. There is a fundamental difference, however, between selection of the employment level and selection of the price level. There are some employment levels, defined as percentages of the labor force, that are definitely better than others. It is better that 96% of the labor force should be employed, than only 80%. One does not have such a gauge for the price level. The virtues or defects of any particular price level are matters of relationships — relations to past price levels, to existing wage levels, and to foreign price levels, and the relations of particular prices to each other.

Probably the most important consideration in the choice of an initial price level is that the price level taken should be consistent with the maintenance of stable high employment. The lower the price level used in calculating the standard national income, the higher the tax rates that will be required. If the price level chosen is too low, the necessary tax rates may so restrict total demand as to make high employment impossible. A process of gradual adjustment may be needed before a tenable price level is determined.

There are great advantages in not changing the assumed price level once the system is in operation. The standard national income, in terms of which tax rates are set, must be simply and objectively determinable. This will be much easier if the same price level is used year after year. Moreover, certain kinds of change in the price level basis would defeat the stabilizing force of the system. For example, an inflationary increase in prices, with employment at a high level, should not be the signal for raising the *assumed* price level. To raise the assumed price level would lead to reducing the required tax rates and thus would feed the inflation. These presumptions do not rule out the possibility that under some conditions revision of the price level basis may be appropriate. But recognition of the value under most conditions of keeping that level stable would restrain arbitrary increases. It would help counteract the temptation that will always exist to raise the assumed price level in order to rationalize popular but economically injurious tax reductions.

WALTER W. HELLER

C.E.D.'s Stabilizing Budget Policy
After Ten Years*

Heller, in the following critical evaluation of the Committee of Economic Development approach, points out that its program is not quite as automatic as is contended. First, the choice of the level of income and employment at which the budget would be balanced or a small surplus achieved is an act of discretion. Also it may be added that the state of the economy at any one time may be such that a chosen high income-employment level may not be obtainable within the framework of a balanced or surplus budget, but that a deficit would be required. The C.E.D. contention is that this possible incompatibility of goals can be overcome by judicious use of other, including especially monetary, policies. Second, the calculation of what level of income would correspond with any given amount of employment and unemployment requires prediction concerning prices, productivity and growth. Third, the decision as to when an inflation or depression is severe enough to warrant discretionary action is clearly an act of judgment. In addition, Heller has a more optimistic opinion of our forecasting ability, although

* Reprinted by permission of the author and the American Economic Association from *American Economic Review* (September, 1957).

recognizing its shortcomings. Further, he argues that because of these very shortcomings, the government should have the flexibility to change its actions, as events prove old forecasts and policies based on them to have been incorrect. Essentially, Heller's main criticism of the C.E.D. program is that it is more rigid and passive than is warranted by the facts of economic life as he sees them. Heller also makes the interesting observation that by emphasizing the burdensome nature of taxes without a corresponding emphasis on the benefits to be derived from government goods and services, the public sector may be too small from the point of view of maximizing satisfaction from private and public goods together. In his view, if some long-run increase in government spending results from the use of compensatory fiscal policy, this may yield an extra unintended bonus as it leads to a better economic mix. This position is in contrast to that of the classical economists, the C.E.D., and others who are firmly convinced that total welfare is generally enhanced by putting checks on government spending, and that this can best be accomplished by having any increase in expenditures matched by an equal rise in taxes.

The year 1957 is an appropriate time to take stock of the prescription of the Committee for Economic Development for the role of federal tax policy in economic stabilization, not only because tenth anniversaries are good occasions for stock-taking, but more important because recent experience in positive monetary and fiscal policy calls into question some of the assumptions and judgments on which CED's "stabilizing budget policy" is based.[1] Recent modifications of the original CED formula, together with CED's current re-examination of its entire monetary-fiscal policy, also suggest that a reappraisal of the stabilizing budget policy may be timely.[2]

[1] The basic document in which the stabilizing budget policy was first enunciated is *Taxes and the Budget: A Program for Prosperity in a Free Economy* (New York, Nov. 1947). Restatements are available in the 16 national policy statements and other pamphlets on fiscal and/or monetary policy issued by CED since 1947. The latest restatement is in *The Budget, the Economy and Tax Reduction in 1956*, issued June 1956. The May 1957 statement, *Tax Reduction and Tax Reform — When and How*, contains no explicit statement or application of the stabilizing budget policy.

[2] Having toiled rewardingly in the CED vineyards as a consultant and tech-

A review of CED's tax policy for economic stability is a review of the dominant theme in postwar fiscal-policy thinking. A dozen years ago, in view of depression and war experience and under the intellectual impact of Keynes, Hansen, and Lerner, it appeared that the discredited dogma of annual budget balancing might be replaced in the affections of most economists — even if not in the halls of Congress and the White House — by a policy of compensatory or functional finance. But instead, by 1949, the doctrine of automatic flexibility largely held sway — a doctrine which confines the role of budget policy in economic stabilization to the contribution it can make within the limits of (1) marginal budget balancing (*i.e.*, matching of new expenditures with new tax revenues even though the budget *as a whole* may be unbalanced except at some agreed high level of national income), and (2) the deficits and surpluses automatically generated by fluctuations in the level of national income (augmented by discretionary changes only in "serious" recessions or inflations).

What turned the main stream of economic-policy thinking so strongly towards automation of fiscal policy? Intellectual antecedents are not hard to find in the writings on built-in flexibility of Gunnar Myrdal, A. G. Hart, Alan Sweezy, Beardsley Ruml, and even Alvin Hansen in the late 'thirties and early 'forties.[3] But what pushed their efforts to the center of the policy stage and led to the de-emphasis of discretionary compensatory finance? Among the factors that played a major role were: (1) the expansion of the federal budget to a size which made automatic flexibility quantitatively important; (2) the shift of emphasis from secular stagnation to the problem of cyclical fluctuations, a shift which gave a higher priority to flexibility and reversibility in policy; (3) the disappointing record of the immediate postwar economic forecasts that seemed to undercut the foundation on which discretionary policy must rest; and (4) the attractions of a budgetary policy based on automaticity and marginal budget balanc-

nical advisor on budgetary policy, and having been among the worshipers at the shrine of fiscal automaticity, I should perhaps note that this reappraisal has not been entirely unagonizing.

[3] For a useful survey of this subject, see N. F. Keiser, "The Development of the Concept of 'Automatic Stabilizers,'" *Jour. Fin.*, Dec. 1956, XI, 422–41. His survey impresses one with the multiplicity of antecedents which provided the raw materials of the CED policy. However, to CED and its present research director, Herbert Stein, must go most of the credit for developing the specific rationale by which fiscal policy could simultaneously serve two masters, *i.e.*, economic stabilization and budgetary discipline.

ing as a pragmatic middle ground on which a consensus of otherwise widely divergent groups might be reached.[4]

Among professional economists, a remarkable degree of consensus on underlying fiscal strategy was, in fact, reached. After issuance of the basic CED statement in 1947 and important further explorations of built-in flexibility and automatic policy by A. G. Hart, Richard Musgrave and Merton Miller, and Milton Friedman, this trend of thinking culminated in the "Princeton Manifesto" of September 1949. In it, 16 economists of such widely differing persuasions as Howard Bowen, Howard Ellis, J. K. Galbraith, James K. Hall, Paul Samuelson, Sumner Slichter, Arthur Smithies, and Jacob Viner agreed unanimously on a set of policies centering on built-in flexibility buttressed by more or less automatic supplements. The essence of their recommendations was embodied in the Douglas subcommittee report early in 1950.[5]

It should be noted that the Princeton statement, for all its automation of fiscal policy, fell short of a complete victory of rules over authority. It left considerable room for discretion in the light of "recent events and the outlook for the near future." For example, it provided that under conditions of unemployment and deflation, tax increases to match new expenditure programs should be suspended until they could be put into effect without impeding recovery. In addition, it urged that the possibilities of "formula flexibility" be explored since automatic flexibility was no more than "a first line of defense." The statement also called for "more strenuous fiscal measures" "where there is a definite expectation, justified by events, of serious recession or inflation . . . ," a prescription which left considerable latitude for differences of interpretation among the signers. Thus, although the Princeton statement represents the high-water mark of the doctrine of fiscal automaticity (among economists, at least), it did not go as far as CED's original stabilizing budget formula in relying on automatic stabilizers.

---

[4] For an analytical discussion of the background, content, and rationale of CED's policy, see Herbert Stein, "Budget Policy to Maintain Stability," in *Problems in Anti-Recession Policy,* Committee for Economic Development (New York, 1954).

[5] Joint Committee on the Economic Report, *Monetary, Credit and Fiscal Policies,* 81st Cong., 2nd Sess., Sen. Doc. No. 129 (Washington, 1950), esp. pp. 11–17. "Federal Expenditure and Revenue Policy for Economic Stability," the statement of the 16 economists who had been convened by the National Planning Association at Princeton (in September, 1949), was published in *Am. Econ. Rev.,* Dec. 1949, XXXIX, 1263–68.

I. THE STABILIZING BUDGET FORMULA AND PHILOSOPHY

The main elements of current CED fiscal doctrine as presented, applied, and modified in a series of policy statements since 1947 may be summarized as follows:

1. *The Balanced Budget Rule.* (a) Tax rates shall be high enough to balance the cash budget at high employment (defined as employment equaling 96 per cent of the labor force) — the rule of "high-level balance";[6] and (b) additional expenditure programs shall be matched by additional taxes (in terms of their high-employment yield) to maintain this balance at high employment — the rule of "marginal budget balancing." These rules also require that cash surpluses generated by economic growth be eliminated by tax reduction.

2. *Automatic Flexibility.* Surpluses and deficits generated by inflationary and deflationary deviations from high employment should be welcomed as stabilizing influences, but tax rates should not be altered to magnify these surpluses and deficits as an offset to moderate economic fluctuations.

3. *Nonautomatic Deviations.* Given severe inflation or unemployment, either at hand or clearly in the offing, discretionary changes in tax rates (and, more reluctantly, in expenditure programs) may be made to enlarge the deficits or surpluses beyond the levels generated by built-in flexibility. Recessions or inflations falling short of this "severe" category may call for some adjustments in the effective dates of tax changes designed to maintain high-level balance.

4. *Other Exceptions.* Large, temporary bulges of expenditures need not be covered immediately by tax increases. Surpluses generated by economic growth or expenditure reductions should not be converted into tax reductions until they are large enough and certain enough "to give room for significant tax reform" without danger of creating deficits during prosperity.[7]

5. *Relation to Other Policies.* "The stabilizing budget policy . . . should be regarded as part of an overall financial policy for greater economic stability, in which not only budget policy but also monetary

[6] The original 1947 formula called for a $3 billion surplus at the agreed high level of employment, but implicitly in 1952 and 1953 and explicitly in 1954, CED changed its fiscal target to a balanced cash budget at high employment. Since the choice of a surplus, balance, or deficit as the high-employment target is an arbitrary one, a more generalized label such as "a fixed revenue-expenditure relationship at high employment" would be more accurate.

[7] CED, *The Budget, The Economy and Tax Reduction in 1956* (New York, 1956), p. 7.

policy, debt management, federal loans and guarantees have important functions."[8]

What assumptions underlie these policy prescriptions? Most basically, CED policy rests on the assumption that human frailties and institutional deficiencies — reflected in imperfections and errors of forecasting, slow-moving executive and legislative processes in taxation, and a tendency of human beings to be timid, unpredictable, and biased towards inflation — make it necessary to utilize automatic rather than discretionary fiscal changes in national stabilization policy. As Herbert Stein put it, "The Committee apparently felt that this plan embodied all that fiscal policy could do — in the existing state of affairs — to maintain stability. While 'stronger' programs could be easily conceived, the Committee argued that these stronger programs are likely to be unstabilizing, because of errors of forecasting, lags, and biases in the decision-making process."[9]

Second, even if human and institutional factors were favorable to countercyclical manipulation of tax rates, the desirable "disciplinary effect" of the marginal-budget-balancing rule would still argue for restricting the ordinary scope of fiscal policy to its built-in flexibility. This restriction permits taxes to play their traditional role as a restraint on expenditures.

CED policy appears to reflect two additional articles of faith. The first is that stabilization policy, if forced to choose, should give a relatively strong guarantee of price stability and a relatively weak guarantee of full employment, lest it promote secular inflation.

The second is that heavy reliance on monetary controls for economic stabilization is desirable not only because of their *effectiveness* as a tool for stabilizing aggregate demand (an economic judgment) but also because their *effects* on resource allocation and income distribution are preferred to those of a more aggressive use of fiscal policy, given our present and prospective tax-expenditure structure (a value preference).

II. THE ISSUES OF NEUTRALITY AND DISCRETIONARY ACTION

In evaluating the stabilizing budget policy, one should be careful to distinguish between true and false issues. In particular, there may have been some misunderstanding on the question of budget neutrality and the role of discretion in CED's policy.

[8] *Ibid.*, p. 6.
[9] Stein, *op. cit.*, p. 87.

Neutrality. First, those who espouse high-level balance and marginal budget balancing cannot claim (nor does CED claim) that a balanced cash budget will be neutral in its impact on aggregate demand at high employment nor that balanced-budget increments will be neutral at whatever level of employment they are introduced. It is not surprising that there should be misunderstanding on this point since a policy designed to run a surplus above a "satisfactory high employment" level and a deficit below that level may *seem* to say that the budget is neutral *at* that level. But several considerations quickly make it clear that balance is not at all synonymous with neutrality.

Only a brief reminder of multiplier theory is needed to establish this point. The somewhat battle-scarred "balanced budget theorem" makes clear (1) that matched increments of taxes and factor-purchase expenditures are very likely, if not certain, to have an expansionary effect, and (2) that this effect will vary with consumption propensities and with government expenditure leakages via imports, purchases of capital assets, and the like.[10] Or, turning from marginal to total budgets in terms of high-level balance, we are long since aware that different types of expenditure activity and different types of revenues may have different multipliers. There is no reason to believe that the multiplied income effects of the two sides of the budget will balance each other just because revenues and expenditures happen to be in balance. Neutrality would require attaching a multiplier to each category of taxes and expenditures and then balancing the two sums of the multiplied products.[11]

At a cruder level of budget definition, one encounters significant year-to-year shifts in budget coverage and timing which upset the relationship between the size of the federal cash surplus or deficit and the size of federal subtractions from or additions to private-income flows. For example, a transfer of the financing of certain farm price-support operations from the budget into the banking system via "cer-

[10] For a good bibliography on the subject and for the latest rounds in the controversy on this theorem, see W. J. Baumol and M. H. Peston, "More on the Multiplier Effects of a Balanced Budget," *Am. Econ. Rev.*, Mar. 1955, XLV, 140–48, and the "Comment" by Alvin Hansen, together with their "Reply," *Am. Econ. Rev.*, Mar. 1956, XLVI, 157–62.

[11] For an interesting attempt to estimate the initial demand effects of various broad classes of federal expenditure and revenues, see Arthur Smithies, "The Impact of the Federal Budget," *Rev. Econ. Stat.*, Feb. 1947, XXIX, 28–31. See also A. H. Conrad, "The Multiplier Effects of Redistributive Public Budgets," *Rev. Econ. Stat.*, May 1955, XXXVII, 160–73.

tificates of interest" reduced recorded federal expenditures and deficits by over $1 billion in fiscal 1954. The "Mills Plan" for speeding up corporate income-tax payments fattened federal receipts by $1 to $2 billion a year for five years without changing corporate-tax liabilities. Year-end manipulations can shift significant amounts of revenues and expenditures from one year to another. For example, the devices of retarding the processing of tax payments and accelerating the payment of certain bills have been used to shift hundreds of millions of dollars of budget surplus from one year into the next. The shifting content of the budget as an economic yardstick of government activity not only interferes with any concept of budget neutrality but poses special problems for the managers of federal fiscal policy. If those managers are tightly tied to a rule of high-level budget balance, they will have less flexibility to adjust tax levels to compensate for these budget vagaries, thereby throwing an added burden on monetary policy as the economic adjuster.

Finally, federal surplus and deficit figures fail to reflect adequately the far-flung federal credit programs, which have an important impact on private income and investment. Budget estimates for 1958 show net expenditures of only $1.4 billion for these programs. Yet total new commitments in the form of loans, investments, guarantees, and insurance will exceed $21.0 billion. Outstanding federal guarantees now cover over $50 billion, or 13 per cent, of total private debt.[12] Although largely outside the budget, federal credit programs have a positive role to play in economic stabilization (as CED policy recognizes).

Discretion. A second issue is that of implicit and explicit discretion involved in the stabilizing budget policy. Can this policy, and does it, live by rules alone? Does it draw a defensible line between rules and authority? Samuelson argues persuasively that there is no such thing as a truly automatic mechanism in fiscal policy.[13] Not only is the mechanism established, continued, modified, and abolished by discretion, which rules out any "notion of a genuine difference of kind" but, more than this, "efforts to establish a logically rigorous difference of degree have not met with success." This does not rule out the pragmatic case for pursuing the kind of discretionary action

[12] The Budget of the United States Government for the Fiscal Year 1958, *Budget Message of the President and Summary Budget Statements* (Washington, 1957), pp. 1103–05.

[13] P. A. Samuelson, "Principles and Rules in Modern Fiscal Policy: a Neo-Classical Reformulation," in *Money, Trade, and Economic Growth* (New York, 1951), pp. 162–66.

which an automatic mechanism provides, but it does do violence to any concept that a non-automatic policy is uncertainly managed by fallible men while an automatic fiscal policy is divinely guided by infallible rules.

There are also many explicitly discretionary features in CED's policy. It is left to human judgment to decide when a recession is so moderate that one leaves tax rates completely untouched, when it has reached the point that makes it advisable to suspend the effective dates of tax increases, and when it is "serious" or "severe" enough (CED does not define these terms) to call for outright compensatory rate changes. There are even more difficult decisions on the inflationary side: when is the revenue surplus clearly a product of economic growth which threatens to retard the rate of further growth, and when is it a welcome contribution (perhaps even too small a one) to the fight against inflation?

CED's fiscal formula provides these general guidelines on a surplus at full employment: if employment does not exceed 96 per cent of the labor force, a substantial surplus signals tax reduction, but if employment rises above 96 per cent, one should hold the tax line against inflation. But what if 96 per cent is just a point on a clearly rising trend of employment, or if it is accompanied by a rising price level? Should one simply project the existing employment and price levels into the future, follow the formula, cut taxes, and leave the rest of the job to monetary policy?[14]

Two considerations suggest that CED's generally affirmative answer is not as doctrinaire as one might infer from overemphasis on

[14] In two recent policy statements (*Tax Policy in 1956,* Dec. 1955 and *The Budget, The Economy and Tax Reduction in 1956,* June 1956), CED interpreted its rule in a setting of roughly 4 per cent unemployment, rising price levels, and prospective budget surpluses of $3 to $4 billion. It called in effect for elimination of the surplus. In its December 1955 statement (p. 5), CED said, "Although the actual figure may turn out to be more or less than this, we believe an assumption that taxes can be cut by $3 or $4 billion is a reasonable basis for considering what kind of a tax reduction program is most desirable." The actual cash surplus for fiscal 1956 was $4.5 billion. In the June 1956 statement (p. 8), CED recommended that decisions on tax cuts (to take effect January 1, 1957) "should be based on a comprehensive, authoritative review of the 1957 budget prospect"; the Budget Bureau's *Mid-year Budget Review* estimated the fiscal 1957 cash surplus at $3.7 billion. Apparently, tax cuts of this magnitude were felt to be justified even in the face of incipient inflation on grounds (a) that the transition from a non-CED policy to the CED formula required elimination of the budget surplus at 96 per cent employment and (b) that additional inflationary pressure generated by moving onto the CED track was to be offset by a tightening of monetary policy, thus combining a less

the automaticity of the stabilizing budget rule. First, in a current study of the problem of inflation, CED is considering this question: does the economic record of the postwar decade establish reliable clues to the "terms of trade" between the level of unemployment and the rate of increase in the price level? Is 4 per cent the magic number that is consistent with a 0 per cent price rise? Or are the terms of trade such that insistence on a 3 per cent unemployment target will bring about a 1 to 2 per cent price rise per annum? Once these terms of trade have been established empirically, of course, one still has to make a choice between the higher level of employment with the greater inflation potential and the lower level with the greater likelihood of price stability.[15]

Second, CED has opened the door slightly to further exercise of discretion in its year-to-year applications of the rule. For example, concern over inflation in 1955 apparently influenced CED's choice among alternative budgetary predictions in a direction indicating no tax reduction at that time, and in 1956 led it to suggest that the effective date of proposed tax cuts be deferred to January 1, 1957.

Given this much discretion in the management of its fiscal formula, why does CED stop so far short of full discretion? Is it justified in assigning to fiscal measures an essentially passive role and to monetary measures a decidedly active role in stabilization policy? The search for an answer leads us to consider the forecasting issue, the relative effectiveness and impacts of monetary and fiscal policy, and the expenditure discipline of CED's budget-balancing rule.

restrictive budget policy with a more restrictive monetary policy. While this was perhaps a correct application of the CED formula (though unemployment figures hovering between 3.2 and 3.7 per cent of the labor force in the last half of 1955 raise some doubts on this score about the late-1955 recommendation), one may question whether it was a wise recommendation in the light of the facts available *at that time* (*i.e.*, not just in retrospect).

[15] Note that CED has long since abandoned its initial 1947–48 position of trying to roll prices back to a pre-existing (lower) level. As introduced in 1947 and applied in recommendations to the Senate Finance Committee in 1948, the CED formula used the early-1947 price level in its calculations of high-employment national income, federal expenditures, and revenues. But by 1949, it became apparent that a roll-back of prices to 1947 would involve severe tax rates and serious threats to full employment. Starting in 1949, CED has employed the current price level as the basis for its calculations. The effect of this is (1) to accept past inflation as a *fait accompli*, but (2) to assume that future inflation will be prevented by appropriate stabilization policy (or by developments in the private economy).

III. ECONOMIC FORECASTING AND DIAGNOSIS IN STABILIZATION POLICY

Deficiencies in our ability to forecast have loomed large in CED's case for automaticity in budget policy coupled with heavy reliance on flexible credit policy.[16] But forecasting is only one element of a broader issue. The question is not merely (a) whether forecasts of future economic conditions are reliable enough to permit discretionary preventive action but (b) whether diagnoses of current business conditions and movements should be used to guide tax and expenditure policies as instruments of discretionary remedial action.[17] CED does not eschew this "comprehensive look" at the economic situation, but, except in severe recession or inflation, it permits only monetary policy to respond to and be guided by the resulting diagnosis.

What conditions would be sufficient to make a defensible case for letting fiscal policy also respond to the "comprehensive look" rather than keeping it on a straight and narrow path with the aid of blinders attached by the CED rule? The first is that information excluded from the decision-making process under the rule would, if granted entry, clearly call for remedial or preventive fiscal action where the CED rule calls for inaction or contrary action. The second is that the information be reasonably complete and reliable.

As suggestive rather than conclusive demonstrations that these conditions may be met, the following four sets of situations which seem to find counterparts in postwar experience may be postulated. All four are presumed to occur in a setting of roughly 96 per cent employment and short of the boundary line labeled "serious inflation."

1. One case combines ample capital capacity, gently rising consumer demand, and strong pressures for public, especially state-local, construction; the other combines limited capital capacity, strong consumer demand, and little pressure for public construction. The first case might well call for credit restrictions, a balanced federal-state-local budget, and some federal tax reductions or tax sharing to put more fiscal resources at the disposal of state-local government; the second suggests less monetary restrictions, federal budgetary surpluses, and less transfer of fiscal capacity to state-local government.

[16] See, for example, CED's *The Stabilizing Budget Policy* (New York, 1950), pp. 5–6.

[17] In putting the point this way, I am not unaware, first, that remedial action for current economic ills must either be appropriate to future economic circumstances or be quickly reversible and, second, that the discussion here sidesteps for the moment the question of how rapidly tax and expenditure policy can respond to the economic information and diagnosis we put at its disposal.

2. In one case the 4 per cent unemployed group consists of regular members of the labor force pressing for a job, while in the other the group consists largely of people who are only loosely part of the labor force (elderly persons, housewives, etc.), and who less adequately satisfy employer needs. The second case may require more restrictive budgetary policy than the first.

3. In one case, "privately financed deficit spending on government account" (e.g., business borrowing to cover construction and production costs incurred on the basis of military orders) may be large and rising as in 1951–52, in another, small and falling, as in 1956–57.[18] The former situation might call for a larger federal surplus, the latter, a smaller one, than CED's rule.[19]

4. Most cases of inflation will satisfy the traditional assumption (accepted by CED) that with stable tax rates and expenditure programs, the federal surplus will automatically grow and thereby dampen inflationary pressures. But the possibility of a disturbing alternative case has been raised by 1957 experience. In this case, the type (or stage) of inflation may be such as to expand federal expenditures for military procurement, public construction, and government salaries faster than federal revenues expand. The resulting decline in the surplus might be the signal for a tax increase if inflationary pressures were diagnosed as persistent.[20]

On the recession side, the need for going behind the aggregates as a basis for determining the appropriate fiscal policy can also be illustrated. R. A. Gordon makes a convincing case for early diagnosis of a moderate downturn to determine whether it is (1) a "pure" minor recession calling for reliance on automatic stabilizers, easy money, and perhaps discretionary action to liberalize unemployment

[18] For a development of this concept and statistical estimates of the magnitudes involved, see A. G. Hart, "Fiscal Policy Implications of Reductions in Appropriations for Fiscal 1958," *Fiscal Policy Implications of the Economic Outlook and Budget Developments: Hearings before the Subcommittee on Fiscal Policy of the Joint Economic Committee* (Washington, 1957), pp. 72–76.

[19] Whether one should consider such induced deficits as a manageable stabilization-policy variable or as part of the complex of developments in the private sector to be counterbalanced, if necessary, by budgetary and monetary policy depends in good part on their controllability. From Hart's analysis one may infer that while they may be controllable by military authorities, they are not likely to be controllable by stabilization authorities.

[20] To test the traditional and alternative assumptions on inflation's budgetary impact calls for analysis and, to the extent possible, measurement of the relative behavior of government resource-using expenditures, transfer payments, and various kinds of taxes under the impact of different types and stages of inflation.

payments and accelerate light public works expenditures or (2) an "intermediate" or "hybrid" recession calling for the "fullest scope of the conventional instruments of stabilization policy. . . ."[21]

The foregoing discussion serves to illustrate the case, conceptually, for discretionary adjustment of fiscal policy to take account of a far broader range of information than is admissible under the CED rule. But one should also confront the forecasting issue on CED's own terms as a basis for preferring its rule to a managed compensatory fiscal policy.

First, managing even an "automatic" budgetary policy involves many explicit and implicit forecasts. To calculate revenues and expenditures under existing programs in terms of the "assumed high level of employment" requires assumptions or projections (forecasts?) of price levels, labor force, and productivity. Projection of the current price level into the future involves obvious hazards, and the jerky rate of gain in productivity (*e.g.*, fast in 1955 and slow in 1956) may make reliance on average rates of gain misleading for any given year. Even more vexing is the forecasting of federal expenditure levels, a vexation that no formula can escape.[22] Recent official budget estimates made well along in a particular fiscal year have turned out to be several billions wide of the mark. It may well be that CED's rule denies the fiscal policy-making process access to other economic variables which can be forecast within ranges of tolerance as narrow as, or even narrower than, those which apply to its budgetary forecasts.

Second, is economic forecasting as slender a reed as it appeared to be 10 years ago? No conclusive evidence is available to prove that forecasting techniques are now a thoroughly reliable basis for discretionary stabilization policy. But many new or improved forecasts of important segments of the economy, such as plant and equipment outlays, are now available. The Council of Economic Advisers does

[21] R. A. Gordon, "Types of Depressions and How to Combat Them," *Policies to Combat Depression,* National Bureau of Economic Research (Princeton, 1956), pp. 13–16. Gordon's analysis leads him to conclude that "Discretionary action, extending beyond the field of merely monetary policy, is necessary in all except relatively pure minor cycles" (p. 12).

[22] CED's formula involves the additional demanding problem of differentiating among (1) those federal expenditure changes which are not to be matched by tax changes, namely, expenditure responses to fluctuations in the level of income and employment; (2) those which are to be matched, namely, the increases or decreases in government programs and the noncyclical expansions or contractions of open-ended programs; and (3) those which fall under the intermediate heading of "large, temporary bulges of expenditure" not requiring fully matching tax increases.

not hesitate to invoke "prospective economic conditions" as a basis for discretionary judgments to hold the line on federal taxes.[23] Qualified observers judge our short-term forecasting record as having operated "not too unsuccessfully" in recent years.[24] Guarded optimism as to the future of economic forecasting seems justified.

Third, it does not *necessarily* follow that present limitations on our forecasting abilities strengthen the case against flexible, discretionary tax action. It can be argued, on the contrary, that these limitations should lead policy-makers to bend every effort to make tax and expenditure devices more readily adjustable to unfolding economic developments.[25] CED prefers monetary policy on this score because it can be "reconsidered, changed, and, if necessary, reversed at short intervals," while tax action tends to be slow, intermittent, and difficult to reverse.[26] More progress might be made in overcoming these defects of the taxing process if reliance on fiscal automaticity and monetary manipulation did not remove some of the pressure for action.

IV. THE RELATIVE ROLES OF FISCAL AND MONETARY POLICY

The presumed operational superiority of monetary over fiscal policy as a flexible stabilization instrument, especially in dealing with inflationary pressure, requires rigorous re-examination in the light of six years of experience with an unleashed monetary policy and the rising tide of informed criticism based on this experience. Since the preference for monetary policy also involves "the diverse values and objectives that move men,"[27] one needs to go beyond questions of effectiveness to questions of effects.

[23] "In view of the budgetary outlook and prospective economic conditions, present tax rates should be continued . . . ," *Economic Report of the President* (Jan., 1957), p. 48.

[24] R. A. Gordon, "Stabilization Policy and the Study of Business Cycles," *Am. Econ. Rev.*, Proceedings, May 1957, XLVII, esp. p. 121.

[25] A. G. Hart (*op. cit.*, p. 73) strongly urges new efforts to develop speedy and reversible tax measures, including intrayear adjustments of the withholding rate, to cope with the difficulties of forecasting budget magnitude, let alone developments in the private economy.

[26] CED, *op. cit.*, 1956, pp. 6–7.

[27] "At any given moment, policy must be based not only on known facts about the nature and operation of the economy, but also on guesses and conjecture and on a balance of the diverse values and objectives that move men," National Bureau of Economic Research, *Financial Research and the Problems of Our Day*, 34th Annual Report (New York, 1957), p. 20.

Time lags. Automatic fiscal stabilizers gain strong support from their superiority with respect to the three familiar lags in stabilization policy: the recognition lag, the administrative lag, and the operational lag. Income-tax collections, unemployment compensation, and similar built-in stabilizers respond promptly to economic events which may take months for the human eye or electric brain to recognize. No legislative or executive body has to intervene to bring them into play. Automatically, the fiscal stabilizers offset between 35 and 40 per cent of a change in gross national product. Yet, while this offset to economic fluctuations is substantial, the effect of automatic stabilizers is more to cushion the shocks of recession and inflation than to set up powerful counterforces. By themselves, they constitute a "tranquilizing budget policy" rather than a truly stabilizing one.

But going beyond these built-in tranquilizers, we promptly come face to face with the issue of the relative behavior of discretionary fiscal and monetary policy in terms of the three lags. This issue, which had in the past been clearly resolved in favor of monetary policy, has been reopened on the basis of new evidence and new thinking. On the recognition lag, both policies suffer the same disability. On the administrative lag, monetary policy clearly carries the day. The basic question is whether its superiority on this score is more than offset by its inferiority in terms of the operational lag, *i.e.*, the length of time between policy action and the effective impact of that action on the economic situation.

In fiscal policy, we are dealing *directly* with income flows, with definitive and direct action to increase or decrease them. But in monetary policy and debt management, we are dealing only *indirectly* with income flows via impacts on liquidity and asset structure. The large cushion of short-term governments in the hands of banks means that the credit reins do not tighten on bank loans until the banks have disgorged these securities over a period of many months after tight-money policies are instituted (and unfortunately for the next period of inflation, experience suggests that the short-term securities flow back to the banks in times of slack loan demand). These and other factors led Warren Smith to conclude that "the operational lag may be considerably longer for monetary than for fiscal policy, at least in many situations."[28]

Further, the administrative lag in taxation need not always be a long one. Under pressure, Congress enacted $5 billion of additional

[28] W. L. Smith, "On the Effectiveness of Monetary Policy," *Am. Econ. Rev.*, Sept. 1956, XLVI, 588–606.

taxes within weeks after the outbreak of war in Korea and rushed through a $1 billion excise tax reduction in one month in 1954. If one were to add to the scheduled federal excise and corporate income tax reductions now on the statute books an individual income tax component, one would have on the shelf three important potential offsets to recession that Congress could put into effect in a matter of days or at most weeks.[29]

Other operational considerations. Without going into detail one may cite other doubts and questions about the effectiveness of monetary policy that have been raised by close students of the subject. Hyman Minsky shows that restrictive central banking measures and rising interest rates generate institutional changes which increase velocity and decrease liquidity and thereby destabilize the money market. He concludes, "The asserted asymmetry of monetary policy (that it is effective in constraining an inflation and ineffective in constraining a depression) is not true; monetary policy is of very limited effectiveness both in constraining an inflation and in counteracting a depression."[30]

Relatively stable tax rates as a favorable factor in business expectations are often cited as one of the important advantages of the stabilizing budget policy. But analyses by Ervin Miller and Alvin Hansen lead to the conclusion that the upsetting expectational effects of the large fluctuations in interest rates and capital values required to stabilize the economy via monetary policy are a high price to pay for more stable tax rates.[31]

Canada's recent experience has revealed distressing limitations to the effectiveness of restrictive monetary policy. As in the United

[29] The Congress in effect created a "shelf" of tax reductions much like the "public works shelf" often urged as an antidepression measure when it legislated automatic expiration dates for some of the tax increases enacted in 1951 (previously March 31, but beginning in 1958, June 30, a date by which the validity of year-end economic forecasts and the nature of the budget picture are much clearer). The conscious development of a broader program of "on-the-shelf" tax reductions has much to commend it. When inflation threatens, the cuts could be postponed as they were in 1955, 1956, and 1957. But when an economic recession or a slowdown of economic growth faces the country, Congress could pull the tax cuts off the shelf or let them come down on the specified date. This would greatly shorten the lag between an economic downturn and positive tax action to counteract it.

[30] H. P. Minsky, "Central Banking and Money Market Changes," *Quart. Jour. Econ.*, May 1957, LXX, 184.

[31] Ervin Miller, "Monetary Policy in a Changing World," *Quart. Jour. Econ.*, LXX, Feb. 1956, 23–43; A. H. Hansen, *The American Economy* (New York, 1957), Ch. 3.

States, these limits resulted partly from sales of government securities by banks and the existence of consumer finance and other credit sources outside of the direct reach of central banking policy. In part, the desire to maintain "orderly conditions in financial markets" played a role.[32]

On recent British experience with monetary restrictions, Warren Smith and Raymond Mikesell conclude that "while some of the weakness of British monetary policy is due to peculiar features of the British economy and its monetary system, the episode is indicative of the general limitations of monetary policy."[33]

The disappointing record of recent monetary restrictionism strongly suggests that monetary policy as a curb on inflation is subject to limitations and side effects to which CED (among many others) did not give sufficient weight in determining its relative reliance on fiscal and monetary measures. If this is true, a reappraisal would logically lead to a shift of emphasis toward discretionary tax and expenditure policy unless it could be demonstrated that the deficiencies of monetary policy are more amenable to correction (perhaps by selective credit controls) than those of fiscal policy.

Value preferences. Evidence on the inadequacies of monetary policy may or may not dislodge some of its advocates from their existing positions, depending on how strongly they prefer the patterns of resource allocation and income distribution (by income brackets as well as social classes) implicit in monetary controls to those implicit in fiscal controls.

The issue was pointedly drawn by Stein and Samuelson recently.[34] While essentially agreeing that we have it within our fiscal-monetary power to achieve reasonable stabilization together with the capital accumulation rate and distributive objectives we desire, they differed sharply in the uses to which they would put monetary and fiscal tools. Stein would use a "faster or slower growth of the money supply" to expand or restrict total demand, thereby allowing us "to

---

[32] Bank of Canada, *Annual Report of the Governor for the Year 1956* (Ottawa, Feb. 1957), esp. pp. 23–36.

[33] W. L. Smith and R. P. Mikesell, "The Effectiveness of Monetary Policy: Recent British Experience," *Jour. Pol. Econ.*, Feb. 1957, LXV, 38.

[34] Herbert Stein, "Stimulation of Consumption or Investment through Tax Policy," pp. 245–49, and P. A. Samuelson, "The New Look in Tax and Fiscal Policy," pp. 229–34, Joint Committee on the Economic Report, *Federal Tax Policy for Economic Growth and Stability*, Papers Submitted by Panelists Appearing Before the Subcommittee on Tax Policy (Washington, November 9, 1955).

determine both the structure of taxes and the total amount of taxes by considerations other than the desired level of total demand" and, in particular, "to choose the tax structure that imposes the least direct interference to investment without fear that such a tax structure may restrict investment indirectly by causing a deficiency of total demand."[35]

In contrast, Samuelson would rely mainly on fiscal policy to control aggregate demand. To achieve the goals of high investment, substantial redistribution, and full employment without inflation, he would (1) make investment funds easy and cheap to get by low interest rates and liberal credit programs; (2) impose progressive taxes, and (3) enact tax increases to produce inflation-curbing surpluses.[36]

The important point here is not to choose between these two alternative approaches, but to make clear that they involve fundamental differences in their impact on the structure of our economy and the distribution of income among different income-size and functional groups. Among the effects of the high-tax low-interest policy, for example, would be (1) to promote government capital formation at the expense of private consumption, (2) to lower the relative rewards for less risky as against more risky uses of money, and (3) to offer a net stimulus to uses (like public construction) which could take advantage of the low interest rates without encountering the high tax rates. The opposite policy, judging by recent experience, tends to pinch particularly hard in the field of state and local construction activities, home building, and small business, without noticeably curbing the business capital-goods boom. This is not to say that one set of effects is "right" and the other "wrong." Rather, it signifies that we have an acute problem of social priorities to resolve before we can come to any consensus on the proper combination of monetary and fiscal policy, and consequently, on the basic question of automatic versus discretionary tax and expenditure policy.[37]

[35] *Ibid.*, p. 248.

[36] *Ibid.*, pp. 232–34.

[37] Smith and Mikesell, *op. cit.*, pp. 38–39, state that "if orthodox monetary policy had been successful in checking inflation in Britain in 1955, it probably would have accomplished this result mainly by causing a reduction in the fixed investment expenditures of the private sector. . . . There is more than one way to control aggregate demand, and monetary policy is not always the best way, even if it works effectively." For a discussion of distributional effects of different policies, see E. R. Rolph, "Economic Stabilization via Taxation, Debt Management, and Monetary Policy," National Tax Association, 1956 *Proceedings* (Sacramento, 1957), pp. 251–57.

V. EXPENDITURE RESTRAINT

Finally, the expenditure-restraining effect of the rule that an additional dollar of expenditures must be matched by an additional dollar of taxes (in terms of the agreed high level of employment) has been one of the CED policy's chief attractions to many groups. Even if the forecasting and timing barriers to compensatory fiscal action could be overcome, preservation of this disciplinary effect would involve severely limiting the scope for countercyclical manipulation of tax and expenditure rates. This raises two important questions. First, does the CED rule effectively restrain spending and promote economy in government? Second, is this restraint a good thing, *i.e.*, does it result in wiser public-expenditure decisions and a better allocation of resources between public and private use, than we would have in the absence of a balanced-budget rule?

As to the first question, we should note that the restraint exerts its force not on those who are pressing for the expenditures but on the President and Congress, whose resistance to pressures is presumably strengthened by the unpleasant political consequences of higher taxes. But one can readily perceive a number of loopholes and bypasses to this restraining effect. For many expenditure programs the initial tax consequences, which are the ones that bear most directly on the political decision, may be only a small fraction of the eventual tax requirements (*e.g.*, the "open-end programs" for farm price supports, veterans benefits, and home mortgage purchases and the large resource development programs like the Missouri basin project). Moreover, there is considerable evidence that when the tax shoe pinches, it tends to jeopardize broad but diffused-interest programs of national significance like aids for school construction or foreign economic aids while exerting little restraint on expenditures infused with a strong sectional interest. The raw pork of the annual rivers and harbors bill gets very little exposure to the heat of the tax fire.

The restraining effect of the tax test may also be undermined by sustained economic growth which automatically increases federal tax revenues by about $3 billion a year. This "easy money" may be an open invitation to added spending.[38]

---

[38] CED's members are not unaware of this problem. A footnote to CED's June 1956, statement (p. 4) severely criticizes the stabilizing budget policy on this score. Perhaps to meet this criticism, J. Cameron Thomson, Vice-chairman of CED, paraphrased the disciplinary rule under present conditions as follows: ". . . every new expenditure program . . . should be undertaken only after the advantages of a tax reduction of similar magnitude are *explicitly* weighed against the need for the new program." "The Realities of Tight Money," an address

The answers to the second question are even less reassuring. Our problem may not be so much that we will fail to count the cost of government expenditures and therefore overexpand government, but that our folkways and fiscal practices tend to discriminate against collective use of resources, even where public use would represent a more efficient resource allocation than private use.[39] Our Puritan insistence on "tax directness" or "tax consciousness" may have had this type of effect. We have failed to distinguish clearly between the two elements of tax consciousness, namely, (1) making the taxpayer aware of his tax payments and (2) making taxes painful to pay. Public goods are not likely to compete on even terms with private goods if taxes are made hard to pay and if taxpayers are made more acutely aware of the tax costs than the service benefits of government.

When economic growth produces slack in the federal budget, the "tax test" does not tell us whether the slack should be taken up by increased federal programs, by increased federal aids to hard-pressed state and local units, by tax reductions to make room for state and local tax increases, or by tax reduction to put money into private pockets. To make these decisions requires a careful balancing of the relative benefits of alternative federal, state-local, or private uses of the funds, not simple reliance on the willingness to bear federal taxes.[40]

Possibly, even if the restraining effect of a balanced-budget rule is weak and often misdirected, the popular devotion to the balanced-budget dogma is so strong that fiscal policy must in some way be accommodated to it. In that case, we might be thoroughly aware of the defects of the rule and yet regard it as a lesser evil than an annually or cyclically balanced-budget rule. But there is a sharp distinction between reluctant acceptance of this rule as a least-evil solution and the implicit suggestion that it represents an optimal solution.

by J. Cameron Thomson, Committee for Economic Development (New York, 1956).

[39] For example, while "extra-buyer benefits" as well as the cost criterion strongly support mosquito-control programs (estimates for area control by local governments against individual or small-group control indicate that the per-person cost of the former may be less than one-tenth of the latter), the adoption of such programs is often thwarted by the attached "mill-levy."

[40] CED's May 1957, statement clearly recognizes this need for developing standards other than the balanced-budget test to determine the worthwhileness of public expenditures. In fact, its discussion of "How to Restrain Expenditures" (op. cit., pp. 8–28) does not base itself on the balanced-budget rule at all, noting that "Even if total expenditures are balanced by receipts, any expenditure is excessive if it costs too much for the national benefit it provides" (p. 8).

And in no event should the rule be allowed to serve, or even to appear, as a substitute for a positive and well-reasoned theory of public expenditures.

VI. CONCLUSION

We are all very much indebted to CED for helping to rechannel public thinking about federal fiscal policy along informed and responsible lines, for stimulating professional fiscal-policy thinking in pragmatic terms, for alerting us to the perils of indiscriminate compensatory fiscal action, and for giving us a periodic perceptive analysis of the tax and budget situation. But the foregoing review offers grounds for skepticism concerning the operational assumptions and conclusions which have led CED to assign fiscal measures an inherently passive role via the stabilizing-budget policy, reserving the active role for monetary controls. If the alternative assumptions and conclusions developed in this paper are acceptable, the practical implication for CED's fiscal-monetary policy is simply this: that its operational effectiveness as an instrument of economic stabilization can be materially improved by increasing its reliance on discretionary relative to automatic fiscal controls and its reliance on fiscal relative to monetary policy.

PART FOUR

BUSINESS OPPOSITION TO
DEFICIT SPENDING

National Association of Manufacturers

Government Spending to Stimulate
Business Activity*

In spite of differences of view and emphasis in the previous selec-
tions, the authors writing in the post-Keynesian period all agree that
the budget need not be balanced annually but should be used to
help offset fluctuations in the private economy even if this entails
deficits in some years. Indeed, one is hard put to find an article by a
professional economist in recent years that will support the balanced
budget principle. Nevertheless, among many nonprofessionals the
notion persists that there is something wrong with unbalanced budgets
and deficit spending. Not all business groups have shared this view;
but one, the National Association of Manufacturers, has consistently

* From *The American Individual Enterprise System* by National Association
of Manufacturers. Copyright, 1947. McGraw-Hill Book Co. Used by permission.

argued in favor of annual budget balancing by the government. As seen in this selection its main argument follows that of the classical economists and rests on the proposition that any policy which permits the government to spend more than it collects in taxes is bound to lead to reckless spending. This is considered a prohibitive price to pay for what, at best, can be a temporary stimulus to the economy. Further, it is argued, deficit spending is a step in the direction of comprehensive planning and with it loss of individual freedom. The argument is aimed not so much against the principles underlying compensatory fiscal policy as it is against what is feared will be the eventual outcome of such policy—growing government and diminshed private enterprise.

1. *Spending Is Like a Virus*

THE first point that may be made in opposition to having the government adopt a deficit spending program as a means of stimulating business activity is that such spending is like a virus in our economic and political system.

Politicians ordinarily like to spend money and hate to impose taxes. This is because spending makes votes, at least for a while, and taxation is likely to lose them. There is an enormous temptation, therefore, once the government starts a deficit spending program, to continue the policy more or less indefinitely. Commitments are made for projects and, once they are started, there is always the powerful argument that they should be completed. One locality or district feels that it has not had its fair share, so there is the demand that this "injustice" be rectified by further spending. A member of Congress facing election finds he is in danger of being defeated, so his party members desire to help him by creating more employment or making more "improvements" in his district. And so on indefinitely. The result is that, once a deficit spending program is started, there never comes a logical and compelling point when it must be stopped. All the arguments and tendencies are on the other side. And this is true regardless of what party is in power and regardless of the particular justification for starting the spending in the first place.

2. *Spending Tends to Frighten Private Investors*

A second argument against deficit spending is that, in an economic system in which private enterprise is the dominating factor, such spending, even in moderate amounts, is likely to frighten business and private investors. The result, therefore, may well be a contraction in private spending more than sufficient to offset the expansion caused by the government spending.

It may be granted that such contraction in private industry is not inevitable. Whether it occurs will depend largely upon the type and extent of the spending, and the political atmosphere in which it is carried out. For example, government spending to build, say, the Panama Canal, or to extend an obviously badly needed highway system, might well be interpreted by the business community and individual investors as a perfectly legitimate outlay about which there was no cause for concern. In consequence, such spending, even though it involved a deficit, probably would have no effect on private investment. On the other hand, an equal amount spent for what is believed to be wasteful purposes, or in an irresponsible way, or in an atmosphere of what appears to be political hostility to individual enterprise, may have exactly the reverse effect and cause a withdrawal of private spending and investment well in excess of the government expenditure. We may get the same effect also if the government expenditure is regarded by business and private investors as constituting a threat of government competition with individual enterprise, or as an entering wedge by government into the fields that heretofore have been regarded primarily as the domain of individual enterprise.

As an instrument of public policy with which to control business activity, therefore, government deficit spending is highly unreliable. It is always necessary to consider the psychological factor, and since this does not lend itself to statistical measurement it is never possible beforehand to be absolutely certain what the result of any given amount of spending will be. For government to adopt such a policy is thus much like a doctor's giving a patient medicine which may act either as a sedative or as a stimulant.

3. *Government Spending Is Relatively Unproductive*

A third argument against government deficit spending is that a dollar of expenditure by government is likely to result initially in a smaller amount of production than will result from a dollar of private expenditure.

Here again this is not necessarily the result. Theoretically, government projects can be financed with the same care and prudence as found in private enterprise. But in practice, as the records clearly show, this seldom works out. In private enterprise there is ordinarily a close connection between those who are spending the money and the source of the money. This creates a certain amount of caution and care in the spending of the money. Of course this is not always true. In many cases in private enterprise there is an enormous amount of waste. But, in the picture as a whole, managers of private enterprise are fairly cautious in their spending. They are cautious because, if their company is to continue to exist in a competitive world, they have to be.

Government employees, in contrast, handle money which does not represent their own savings or the savings of others whom they have succeeded in getting as their financial partners. Because of this and because there is always more money where the first came from, there is a tendency to be more lavish in expenditures, to be less careful of the pennies. Governmentally constructed plants are thus likely to be expensive plants and governmentally managed production is likely to be high-cost production. The public, as a general rule, therefore, gets less production in return for a dollar spent by government than from a dollar spent by private enterprise, and the asset value created by the spending is likely to be less than the money spent, or liabilities incurred, in the creation of the assets.

4. *Deficit Spending Leads to Financial Difficulties*
Fourth, if deficit spending is engaged in persistently and extensively, it is certain in due time to plunge the government into serious financial difficulties.

A government cannot continue indefinitely to run at a deficit without creating an inflationary trend which in time undermines public confidence in its obligations. If this stage is reached, it means that the savings of the thrifty in the form of life-insurance policies, bank deposits, etc., are endangered and perhaps wiped out. It means also that the commercial banks of the country, because they will have to take over increasing amounts of government bonds to finance the deficit, sooner or later become dependent upon government and thereby lose that freedom of action which is essential to the Individual Enterprise System.

How long deficit financing must be continued in order to bring about these results, or what the deficits must amount to in terms of money, are questions which no one can answer. The loss of confidence in the currency or in the obligations of government, like the loss of confidence in the soundness of a bank because of rumors as to its financial position, is a psychological phenomenon. The only safe course for the government to pursue, therefore, is to make certain that its financial policies are such that there can be no possible ground for such loss of confidence.

If the government does not pursue such confidence-inspiring policies, it means that at any time a wave of fear may sweep over the public which will create a financial crisis and perhaps lead to a financial collapse. The mere realization that such an eventuality is possible, too, it should be noted, is certain to have an adverse effect upon the willingness of private investors to risk their funds in new enterprises. Under such conditions investors will tend to keep their funds in the most liquid forms possible — in cash, or in securities of large, highly regarded companies for which there is a ready market. Even though a spending policy may never actually lead to a collapse, the fact that the program being followed makes such a collapse a possibility hinders the orderly, sound development of the economic system.

5. *Spending Must Ultimately Lead to Higher Taxes*

A fifth argument against government deficit spending as a means of increasing the volume of business activity, is that such spending, unless it is to end in national bankruptcy, must ultimately lead to higher taxes in order to carry the interest payments on the increased public debt.

Such increased taxes mean (1) that employers and investors in private industry will have less money than otherwise with which to buy privately produced commodities and services or to make investments in old or new plants, and also that business enterprises will have less funds than otherwise for working capital and plant expansion. (2) The increased taxes are almost certain to fall most heavily upon those groups which, because of their higher incomes, do most of the saving. There will thus be a smaller volume of funds available for investment. (3) Such increased taxes mean that there will be less incentive for those who have surplus funds to invest such funds in private enterprise, and thereby create employment, since with the higher taxes the income which will remain to investors will be lower than otherwise. (4) With less employment there will be a smaller proportion of the public able to pay taxes, and conversely a larger proportion to be supported by public funds.

6. *Spending Discourages Private Saving*

A sixth objection to government deficit spending — one which is closely related to the point just made — is that, when there is such spending, government almost inevitably will attempt to force the interest rate down to artificially low levels. This tends, at least to some degree, to lessen the incentive of individuals to save and thus prevents needed capital formation. Furthermore, such lower interest rates reduce the revenues of endowed institutions and hence undermine the financial position of universities, hospitals, research organizations, etc. Finally, such low interest rates tend to make the return on investments so meager that it is impossible for the thrifty to accumulate funds sufficient to provide the income needed to take care of their old age.

It may be argued, of course, that actually there is no necessity that deficit financing be accompanied by the forced reduction of interest rates to artificially low levels and thus have these undesirable effects. Again, although that is true theoretically, it is not to be expected in practice. When the government has large deficits year after year, it is almost certain to try to drive down the rate of interest at which it can borrow. It does this, not only in order to hold down the aggregate interest charge, but as well because interest payments on government obligations for the most part go to banks and the more well-to-do members of the community, and so are open to political attack. As a practical matter, therefore, it is safe to say that a large deficit spending program by government will always be accompanied, as long as the government can control the money market, by low rates of interest.

7. *Spending Does Not Create Enduring Prosperity*

Seventh, government deficit spending is ordinarily less conducive to enduring prosperity than business activity resulting from private production.

Government deficit spending, granted the purpose is merely to increase the volume of business activity and not to destroy the system of individual enterprise, tends to be based upon decisions far removed from the market place and from the driving power of competition. The government, in a deficit spending program, has as its principal objective the getting of money into the hands of the public and the creation of jobs. Its objective, unless it is attempting to replace private enterprise, is not the production of something for which there is a demand and which can be sold at a price sufficient to cover the costs of production and still leave something over as interest on the capital investment. In other words, by the very nature of the case, a government deficit spending program is designed primarily as a stimulant, not as something which can stand on its own feet and produce a profitable return year after year and decade after decade.

Again, it may be argued that this is not necessarily true, and that is correct. We have had examples of government enterprises operated on sound principles and truly self-supporting. But they have been the exception, not the rule. Usually, governmentally operated enterprises run at a deficit, and ordinarily this is true even though such enterprises are freed of many charges, notably taxes, which are imposed upon private organizations. Taking the record as a whole, therefore, there is little room for doubting that production for the market by private enterprise under competitive conditions is a much greater assurance of enduring prosperity than the spending of any equivalent amount of funds by government.

8. *War Spending No Argument for Peacetime Spending*

Eighth, the fact that large government spending during the war created full employment does not indicate that a spending program during peacetime would have the same result.

During wartimes government provides a virtually unlimited market for the products of a major portion of industry. Further, this market is assured at a price level which makes costs of secondary importance, for in war the primary consideration is to get the needed material more or less regardless of cost. Finally, when millions of men are taken into the armed forces, this curtailment of the labor supply, in combination with the necessity of getting military supplies and the willingness to pay almost any price for them, causes business to bid for labor and accept a degree of inefficiency which at other times would be ruinous.

In peacetimes none of these conditions would prevail even though the government adopted a large spending program. In other words, in peacetimes, although as a result of government spending there may be a large volume of purchasing power in the hands of the public, business has to produce for "the market," not just for a single buyer who cares little about costs. This means that every producer has to compete with every other producer, and hence the efficiency of his production becomes a primary consideration. Instead of being able to bid higher and higher for more and more inefficient labor, therefore, there are definite limits beyond which he cannot go in the way of wages, and if labor is not available at this price he cannot increase employment. In short, under peacetime conditions, government spending, instead of "forcing" full employment in private industry, may well create conditions which make such full employment impossible.

9. *Spending Leads to the Loss of Freedom*

Finally, and in some respects the most important of all the arguments against government spending, a policy of continued deficits on the part of the government must mean ultimately the elimination of competition and the loss of that freedom of choice which is characteristic of a system of democracy and individual enterprise.

This point recently was discussed at length in a series of notable articles by the London *Economist,* which formerly had looked with considerable favor on spending as a means of assuring full employment. According to the *Economist:*[1]

The state's difficulties in entering competitive spheres naturally lead it to concentrate its "public works" in fields that are not financially remunerative, such as public buildings, roads, bridges, and the like. These things are necessary and desirable and they yield nonmonetary dividends; but if too much of the community's savings are invested in forms that yield no money return, there will be trouble. The individuals who save do so in the expectation of monetary return on their savings. A man who has saved all his life cannot live on the magnificence of the local Town Hall or on the smooth directness of the nearest by-pass. If the standard of material living is to maintain its steady rise, it is essential that as much as possible of the community's savings should be invested in forms that will yield a tangible and material dividend in the future — and that is what any state short of the totalitarian has difficulty in doing. Totalitarianism is, indeed, the ultimate end of a "public works" policy, for if any departments of the community's economic life are to be kept independent of the state (whether or not they are collectively owned) it is imperative that they should be constantly reinforced by a stream of new capital investment.

This view also finds expression among the spending advocates of this country. Thus it is said that the control would have to include Congressional delegation of the power of taxation to the group in charge of the spending program. This, for example, is the view of Prof. Alvin Hansen, who says:[2]

Congress should set up a long-run fiscal program adequate to cope with the defense and post-defense problems. Such a program calls for a

[1] London *Economist,* Oct. 10, 1942, p. 439.

[2] Alvin H. Hansen, *Fiscal Policy and Business Cycles,* 1941, pp. 447–448.

comprehensive, long-range plan. For one thing, Congress should establish a Monetary and Fiscal Authority. Such an authority should be assigned the responsibility of advising and recommending to the Executive with respect to the implementation of a comprehensive tax program. The Executive, acting under the advice of the Monetary and Fiscal Authority, should be empowered to increase or curtail at the appropriate time a special category of public improvement expenditures, designed to promote employment stability and expansion. He should, moreover, be empowered, with the advice of the Monetary and Fiscal Authority, to determine the imposition and withdrawal of taxes designed to check inflation or deflation and to change existing rates within the limits imposed by the comprehensive tax program. Congress might specify certain criteria which the Monetary and Fiscal Authority would be required to take cognizance of in the determination of the appropriate timing of such adjustments. The determination ought certainly to be discretionary, but it is possible that the objective criteria could be sufficiently definite so that limits could be imposed upon the range within which discretion could be exercised. Upon such determination and proclamation by the Executive the respective provisions of the comprehensive tax measure previously passed by Congress would become effective.

Admittedly, Congress may be reluctant to delegate power to the Executive on so vital a matter as the timing of the application of tax rates and expenditures. But, if we are to make the economy workable under modern conditions, it will be necessary to engage in bold social engineering, and especially is this true with respect to the defense program and its aftermath.

Believers in democracy and individual enterprise are unable, of course, to go along with any policy that would lead to the sacrificing of such basic rights of the individual — rights guaranteed by the Constitution and the very foundation of our form of government. They are unwilling to turn over the welfare of our 140 million people to the whims of a small clique of "planners" and politically appointed bureaucrats, for they know that it is not possible to have individual freedom and bureaucratic dictation simultaneously. They know that under such conditions all individual freedom ultimately must disappear.

SIDNEY S. ALEXANDER

Opposition to Deficit Spending for the Prevention of Unemployment*

As observed earlier, the preceding article by the National Association of Manufacturers presents a firm position against unbalanced budgets that is rarely found among economists. If the economics profession, instead, generally agrees that compensatory fiscal policy, which will likely include periods of deficit spending, is a useful instrument for promoting prosperity, it may well be asked why conservative groups like the National Association of Manufacturers should be opposed. After all, its membership is composed of firms which can only benefit by sharing in prosperity, whether caused by successful fiscal policy or other factors. Sidney S. Alexander, in his attempt to answer this question, suggests that if the businessman accepts the principle of government responsibility for maintaining prosperity, it, in effect, is an acknowledgment that private enterprise cannot do the job; this heightens the role of government and shrinks that of business in our socio-economic system. If this view of the businessman's prime concern is correct, it may well be that whatever controversy over the stabilizing use of fiscal policy remains is due not so much to disagreement over its economic soundness as it is to fear of the possible non-economic repercussions, in large part unknown, yet vividly and somberly imagined.

I. THE PROBLEM AND METHOD OF APPROACH

THE theory supporting deficit spending for the prevention of unemployment is that widespread unemployment arises from a defi-

* Reprinted by permission from *Income, Employment and Public Policy: Essays in Honor of Alvin H. Hansen* (W. W. Norton and Co., New York, 1948).

ciency in aggregate demand. Deficit spending by government, financed by the creation of credit, then works toward the alleviation of unemployment not only through the direct employment of workers for producing the objects of government expenditure, but also through the secondary or multiplier effects of the additional expenditures of those who receive payment from the government in the first instance.[1] The deficit spending theory has associated with it an important assumption of fact, namely, that under normal conditions in advanced countries, especially the United States, present relations of productive capacity and income distribution would lead, if full employment were achieved, to a tendency for savings of individuals and corporations to exceed expenditures of individuals and corporations from sources other than income. Under these conditions full employment cannot be expected unless a government deficit makes up the difference.

If this theory and these facts are true it would certainly seem to be in the interest of all concerned for the government to ensure full employment by the appropriate amount of deficit spending when necessary. The fact that an important segment of our society is vehemently opposed to deficit spending as a cure for unemployment must then require some explanation. It is especially important to determine the basic attitudes and beliefs on which opposition to deficit spending rests, so that it may be possible to judge whether or not this opposition may be overcome in the future, either by education and propaganda on the one hand, or by the impact of the brute fact of depression on the other.

In considering the opposition to deficit spending, it is not proposed here to evaluate the merits of the arguments advanced on either side, since it is by now clear that many of the arguments are merely rationalizations of attitudes based on the economic or social position of the person concerned. It is fairly obvious that the lines between protagonists and antagonists in the majority of cases follow lines of class or political stratification. Broadly speaking, business men and conservatives are against deficit spending, trade unionists and liberals are for deficit spending. The main focus of our problem is accordingly why business men and those politicians who represent the business man's point of view are opposed to deficit spending as a means for preventing unemployment, even though according to the deficit

---

[1] Actually some stimulation of employment is to be expected from increased government spending, even if financed out of taxation, but this is a finer point which need not concern the argument here.

spending theory the business man would presumably be better off under deficit spending.

In the following discussion it is assumed that the deficit spending theory is valid, and that unemployment, otherwise inevitable, can be avoided by a government program of deficit spending. Opposition in this case may be based first of all on misunderstanding. It may not be realized by the average business man that deficit spending can prevent unemployment, or that unemployment is inevitable without deficit spending.

Alternatively, even though it is realized that deficit spending is necessary for the achievement of full employment, there may be good reasons for business men to dislike full employment. They may particularly fear the deterioration in the discipline of the working force that comes about as a result of full employment. Similarly, with full employment the bargaining power of labor can be expected to improve so that there may be adverse effects of full employment upon the share of the employer in the total product. In short, business men may be interested in the maintenance of a pool of unemployed in order to protect worker discipline and to prevent wage rises. We may refer to this possibility as the "industrial reserve army" basis of opposition to deficit financing.

Another possible basis for opposition derives from the class aspect of the deficit financing program. Deficit financing first gained prominence in this country as a means of curing unemployment as part of the New Deal, which also contained broad measures favoring the economic status of industrial workers and farmers. In general, full employment programs, and especially those based on deficit financing, have been most closely identified with the interests of the urban proletariat, so that some of the opposition may be explained by this identification. This we may call the "class antagonism" aspect of opposition to deficit financing.

Finally, and certainly very important, is the fear of increasing state power that is associated, at least in the minds of business men, with government action to relieve unemployment, especially if that action takes the form of deficit spending. This fear leads to the vigorous defense of the free private enterprise system against the threats of statism, socialism, totalitarianism, and deficit spending.

We shall consider each of these four possible bases of opposition in turn: (1) misunderstanding; (2) industrial reserve army; (3) class antagonism; (4) fear of increasing power of the state. Each of these attitudes will be examined in order to evaluate its actual importance as a basis of opposition and to judge the probability that it may be changed in the future.

II. THE FULL EMPLOYMENT BILL

The analysis is based principally on the arguments and attitudes displayed in the public controversy centering around the proposed Full Employment Bill of 1945 which became the Employment Act of 1946.[2] The essential features of the original bill were: (1) A forthright declaration of policy affirming the fostering of free enterprise, the right to work, and the responsibility of the U.S. Government to assure opportunity for full employment, first by stimulating private and non-Federal investment and expenditure, and then by providing such volume of Federal investment and expenditure as may be necessary for full employment. (2) A provision for a National Budget to be submitted by the President to each regular session of Congress. The National Budget was to contain estimates, for the next fiscal year or longer, of the labor force, of the volume of total investment and expenditure required to keep that labor force employed, and of the expected total investment and expenditure from all sources private and public. If a deficiency of total expenditure and investment below that required for full employment was expected, the President was to propose measures for stimulating private investment and expenditure. If this stimulation could not be expected to make up the deficiency, the President was to propose increased Federal investments and expenditure to bring the expected total up to that level required for full employment.[3]

The bill did not itself provide for deficit financing, but in essence directed the President to propose increased government expenditure and investment when required for full employment, and this could

[2] An account of the early history of the measure up to its consideration by the Senate Banking and Currency Committee starting July 30, 1945 can be found in *Hearings before a Subcommittee of the Committee on Banking and Currency,* United States Senate, Seventy-Ninth Congress, First Session, on S. 380, Washington, 1945, pp. 10–17. This volume is hereafter referred to as Senate Hearings. Further public discussion of the Full Employment Bill is to be found in *Hearings before the Committee on Expenditures in the Executive Departments,* House of Representatives, Seventy-Ninth Congress, First Session, on H.R. 2202, Washington, 1945. This volume will be referred to as House Hearings.

[3] There were also inverse measures in case an inflation threatened, but those do not concern us here.

reasonably be expected to involve deficit spending. But the term "deficit spending" is so unpopular politically that the proponents of the bill hotly denied that it was based on the theory of deficit spending. In fact the history of the bill presents a fine example of a semantic stalemate. The supporters of the bill dared not come out point-blank for deficit spending because the term is too offensive to the general mores. But on the other hand the enemies of the bill could not very well go on record as opposing a measure entitled a "Full Employment Act." The Employment Act of 1946 as finally passed accurately reflects the working out of this dilemma. The Act was a manifesto and the Congress was not willing, under the conditions of employment and public opinion of February 1946, to sign so vigorous a manifesto as was contained in the original bill. The great scare about immediate post-war unemployment had considerably subsided by February 1946, but at an earlier date — September 1945 — when the fear of immediate post-war unemployment was still strong, the Senate did pass by a vote of 71 to 10 a version of the Full Employment Act, which, though considerably modified from the original bill, still preserved the main framework.[4] It contained the words "investment" and "expenditure," "full," "assure," and for "right to employment" substituted the weaker though still vigorous phrase "are entitled to an opportunity for . . . employment." The near unanimity in the passage of the bill in the Senate was obtained principally by two qualifications. The first was that Federal responsibility and action for full employment should be "consistent with the needs and obligations of the Federal Government and other essential considerations of national policy."[5] The second was that any program for Federal investment and expenditure for the fiscal year 1948 or after, in peacetime, should be accompanied by a tax program over a reasonable period of years such that there would be no net increase in the national debt. In short, the deficit financing was to be compensated by surpluses in subsequent years.

An employment act was finally passed, but one completely purged of the fighting words: "investment and expenditure,"[6] as in "such Federal investment and expenditure as will be sufficient to bring the aggregate volume of investment and expenditure by [all sources] up to the level required to assure a full employment volume of production"; "full," as in "full employment"; "guarantee" and

---

[4] House Hearings, pp. 4–7.

[5] S. 380, Section 2d (4), reprinted in House Hearings, p. 5.

[6] Cf. S. 380 (original draft), Section 3c, reprinted in Senate Hearings, p. 7.

"assure," as in "assure or guarantee the existence of employment opportunities"; "right," as in "the right to employment."[7]

Nevertheless, the Act as passed permits the President to do anything that the original bill directed him to do. In fact, the opponents of the original bill were fond of insisting that there was nothing in that bill that the President could not already do without the bill. Although the Act as passed is no weaker than the original bill in the powers it gives to the President, it is weaker in the language it uses and in the remedies it suggests. The importance of passing a bill was to put the government on record as taking responsibility for the prevention of unemployment, using deficit spending if necessary. The language of the Act, although qualified, does put the government on record as responsible to do *something* about unemployment. With a given Congress and a given President, the program that will be suggested in the President's Economic Report and the resulting program adopted by Congress cannot be expected to be different from the corresponding programs that would be forthcoming under the National Budget as originally specified.

The fact that the bill went through several stages of amendment and attenuation before it was passed served as an experiment to determine the critical point at which opposition turns into acquiescence. The following analysis of the various possible bases of opposition derives most of its materials from the controversy centering around the measure in its various forms.

III. MISUNDERSTANDING

The most obvious explanation of the paradox that business men and others are opposed to deficit spending even though it is in fact good for them is that they do not understand the situation. This misunderstanding may be buttressed by a set of attitudes derived from the rules of personal finance that are inapplicable to government. We may call such an extension of individual standards to government finance the anthropomorphic fallacy. A somewhat more sophisticated type of disagreement arises from a rejection of the premise on which the theory of deficit spending is based. It is contended that our economic system, especially if the government would only leave it alone, would have a natural tendency to approach a state of full employment. An even

---

[7] The House representative on the joint conference which composed the final text of the bill boasted of these verbal purges in his report to the House. Congressional Record, Seventy-Ninth Congress, Second Session, p. 944.

more sophisticated type of opposition arises from the acceptance of the premise that unemployment is likely, but the rejection of the argument that deficit spending is the cure. We may term these bases of opposition rejection of the premise and rejection of the argument respectively.

By far the most widespread popular opposition to the theory of deficit spending arises from the extension to the government of the canons of sound personal finance. So universal is this attitude that it is not usually necessary to make the argument explicit. Merely to state that a particular measure will increase the national debt is to castigate it, and make it politically difficult to support. This is the reason for the oft-repeated denial by the supporters of the Full Employment Bill that it was a deficit spending measure. The opponents were fond of quoting Franklin D. Roosevelt to the effect that "the credit of the family depends chiefly on whether that family is living within its income, and that is equally true of the Nation."[8]

Universal as is the appeal of the anthropomorphic argument, it must be discounted as a long-run basis of opposition to deficit spending. It can, however, be expected to persist as an auxiliary prejudice whose retention is convenient for those who oppose deficit spending for other reasons. It will also long constitute one of the strongest semantic weapons of the enemies of deficit spending in their appeal to the general public.

The economist's rejection of the anthropomorphic fallacy as a fundamental ground for opposition is based on the ease with which this fallacy is overcome on the part either of disinterested individuals or those who can especially expect to benefit from full employment brought about by deficit spending. It is not in general true that liberals are spendthrifts and conservatives are thrifty, but rather that the former have come to draw a distinction between government debt and individual debt, and the latter still find it convenient not to do so. It is no more likely that the anthropomorphic fallacy will yield before the Keynesian truth, than it was for the protectionist fallacy to have

---

[8] Franklin D. Roosevelt, speech at Pittsburgh, Pa., 1933, quoted by Rep. Woodruff in Congressional Record, Jan. 25, 1946. Other examples are: "For individuals and for government, thrift is the best policy." (John D. Rockefeller, quoted in *Reader's Digest,* Jan., 1945, p. 41.) "The national debt is a burden of over two thousand dollars on every man, woman and child in America. Deficit spending puts further burdens on unborn generations." "I can't spend my way to prosperity, you can't do it, and Uncle Sam can't do it." "Hard work and production make for wealth and prosperity, and not the handing out of borrowed money by the government."

yielded before the truth of the Manchester school. To the degree that the fallacy does support other, better-founded attitudes it may be expected to persist. It accordingly has little independent significance, even though it will live on where its acceptance is derived from more fundamental attitudes.

It was almost uniformly charged by the opponents of the Full Employment Bill that it reflected a lack of confidence in the American system of free private enterprise.[9] This implies, on the part of the opponents of the bill, confidence in the ability of our economic system to function without serious unemployment — an attitude which, of course, requires considerable reconciliation with the occurrence of previous depressions. The reconciliation was most frequently made by the addition of the qualification "if the government only leaves business alone." In fact, the most typical attitude taken by the representatives of business, testifying concerning the Full Employment Bill, was that if government really wanted full employment it would create an atmosphere in which business could go ahead. This "atmospheric" theory of government relations with business particularly stressed "economies in government operations, reduction of taxes, elimination of regimentation, with encouragement of business enterprises large and small."[10] President Mosher of the National Association of Manufacturers indicated that only three developments can bring prosperity to a halt: (1) "Mismanagement of the money and credit system . . ." (2) "Granting or perpetuation of special privileges . . ." (3) "Prevention of an adequate flow of capital into productive, job-making activities."[11] Freely translated, the first point is a demand for sound money, the second for amendment of the Wagner Act in order to put greater responsibility on trade unions. The third point might seem to leave some room for the theory of deficit spending, but Mr. Mosher means by it principally the unfavorable effect of taxation on investment.[12] All three of these possibilities are thus ways in which ill-advised governmental policies can adversely affect business. In its most prevalent form, then, the rejection of the premise is part of a broader argument

[9] See especially the testimony of Ira Mosher, President, National Association of Manufacturers, Senate Hearings, pp. 460 et seq., House Hearings, pp. 573 et seq. See also statements of twenty-five State Chambers of Commerce, House Hearings, pp. 445–457.

[10] Statement by Robert B. Heppenstall, President, Pennsylvania State Chamber of Commerce, House Hearings, p. 454.

[11] House Hearings, p. 548. This argument was included verbatim in the 1947 policy statement of the NAM. See New York Times, Dec. 8, 1946, p. 9.

[12] As indicated in detail in his testimony, House Hearings, pp. 550–551.

against government interference with business. It can therefore most appropriately be considered in Part VI below, where fear of the increasing power of the state is discussed.

In response to the question of whether the atmosphere for business was not satisfactory in the period immediately preceding 1929, the opponents of deficit spending would frequently abandon the rejection of the premise, or would modify the atmospheric theory. When the rejection of the premise was abandoned, the argument was usually advanced that "certainly, you can have full employment under a totalitarian system, but not under a system of free private enterprise," and "unemployment is the price we pay for freedom."[13] The alternative was to modify the atmospheric theory of government relations to business to the extent of blaming the depression of the thirties not so much on government policy as on particular maladjustments not curable by deficit spending. The first way out again leads to the subject matter of VI, namely the fear of increasing the power of the state. The second alternative is in essence a rejection of the argument rather than of the premise, and will be considered under that heading.

A rather curious attitude is often evinced when an opponent of deficit spending theory is forced to accept the premise of the prospect of unemployment. He frequently then states a strong preference for unemployment relief rather than government investment and expenditure for goods and services. This attitude was so general among opponents of the Full Employment Bill that it must be attributed to a fundamental premise of their position. It is probably related to class antagonism, the industrial reserve army, and fear of government power, discussed below.

Since rejection of the premise is a question of fact, can it not be expected that further experience, say of the next depression, will transform this attitude into a recognition of the desirability of deficit spending? In short, is this not merely an example of cultural lag, with the adjustment inevitable but delayed? The greater willingness of British business men to accept a full employment program may be cited as evidence in the affirmative. The only notable degree of acceptance of the deficit spending theory by American business men is among retail trading establishments, especially small ones. Even here the acceptance is far from universal. The most conspicuous business group which has acknowledged the tendency of the economic system to be subject to unemployment for lack of sufficient investment, and

---

13 See, for example, Virgil Jordan, *Full Employment and Freedom in America,* New York, Controllers Institute of America, 1945.

has not ascribed that lack of investment entirely to the adverse influence of government policies on business, is the Committee for Economic Development. In this case the immediate reaction is to reaffirm business' ultimate ability to ensure full employment, but to stress the fact that a conscious and coordinated effort in that direction is necessary. Should this effort on the part of business men prove insufficient to maintain full employment, it is at least somewhat doubtful whether there will be a large scale conversion of the business men with CED to the support of government deficit spending. Rather it is more likely that the impact of continued unemployment on the "enlightened" members of the business community will be to push them further toward a rejection of the argument, a direction already taken by some of their spokesmen who are most conversant with the study of economics.

By far the most common form of rejection of the argument that deficit spending can cure unemployment has already been given in the section on the anthropomorphic fallacy: neither an individual nor a government can spend his way to prosperity. Another type of rejection arises from a misinterpretation of the argument.

Chairman Manasco of the House Committee on Expenditures in the Executive Departments never tired of asking witnesses whether they thought that if the unemployed numbered eight million the Federal government could long continue to pay them each two to three thousand dollars a year.[14] Oddly enough, nobody ever replied to him with a statement of the theory of the multiplier. In view of the rather technical nature of the theory of deficit spending, it is not surprising that many of its opponents should think of it as implying that the government hires all of the unemployed. The ignoring of secondary effects is especially likely when the pump-priming theory is denied, even by those supporting deficit spending. When secondary employment effects are ignored, and a dole is assumed, deficit spending is regarded as a method of taking away from those who produce to give to those who don't. This process, it is held, does not increase the real national income, because work and not deficit spending does that. This particular attitude may have been especially important in affecting the fate of the Full Employment Bill in the House of Representatives, but it is not likely to have much general significance for the future development of attitudes toward deficit spending. It should rather be considered as an appeal to the anthropomorphic fallacy, whereby ignoring of secondary effects permits the use of a

---

[14] House Hearings, pp. 70, 513, 535, 559, 595, 751, and elsewhere.

larger and more intimidating figure for the growth of the national debt.

A more significant type of rejection of the argument, though possibly less important politically in the recent past, is the contention that deficit spending is not a panacea. This position is taken by business men and their representatives who are rather sophisticated students of economics, and it is the most frequent attitude of professional economists who oppose deficit spending. It was probably given fullest expression by George Terborgh: "We do not question that compensatory fiscal policy may provide at times a useful, and even necessary, measure of contracyclical action . . . It would be the grossest self-deception, however, to think that we have at present either the knowledge, the experience, or the institutional mechanisms to apply this weapon in a closely controlled and scientific manner. To conceive of this device as a simple and all-sufficient mechanical solution for our economic ills is simply naive." "Since this idea is a delusion, if we are to maintain a free economy, talk of a right to a job, unless discounted simply as demagogic eyewash, is cruel deception."[15] The line of argument is that unemployment is the result of a number of things, and deficit spending can't overcome many of these things.

Since Mr. Terborgh's position is based on a very high degree of economic competence, it may be taken as the most likely direction in which the attitudes of business men will move under the impact either of education by propaganda or of education by hard knocks in the next depression. In Mr. Terborgh's case this attitude led to a recommendation for a full employment bill with exactly those features that were finally enacted in the Employment Act of 1946.[16] It may accordingly be concluded that a good deal more education of the business man, even by the experience of another depression, may not convert him to the theory of deficit spending for the relief of unemployment.

Rejection of the argument on rational grounds characterized the reception of Keynesian doctrines among economists, but after further discussion this yielded to a broad measure of acceptance. Business men are not so likely to change their views in a similar manner since their opposition is probably based upon more deeply seated grounds than rational analysis of the theory. In the quotation from Terborgh given above it is interesting to note that his denial of the notion that

[15] George Terborgh, *The Bogey of Economic Maturity,* quoted in House Hearings, p. 604, and Terborgh's testimony, p. 607.

[16] House Hearings, pp. 613, 614.

deficit spending will bring full employment is qualified by the reservation "if we are to maintain a free economy." It may be inferred that more fundamental than the rational rejection of the argument is the businessman's fear of growing state power discussed below.

IV. INDUSTRIAL RESERVE ARMY

It is, of course, possible that deficit spending as a means of achieving full employment is opposed because full employment itself is not desired. The supporters of the Full Employment Bill were quick to accuse their opponents of this motive.[17] The contention is that, under conditions of full employment, management has a difficult time keeping labor under its control and labor will be in a better position to get a larger share of the total product. Naturally no opponent of the Full Employment Bill put himself clearly on record as being against full employment, although an occasional remark may be so interpreted. It was very common, however, for enemies of the bill to deplore the effect of passage of the act upon the behavior of workers. An assurance of a right to a job, it was contended, would undermine the incentive to work and would disrupt the functioning of the economy. It is easy to see that this is consistent with a feeling that full employment may be too much of a good thing. There may well be a level of employment below full employment that brings maximum returns to the business man. A large number of the opponents of the Full Employment Bill believed that it would strengthen the feeling among the workers "that the world owes them a living, and through their government they will get it whether they work or not. There ought to be some fear of loss of job to influence this type of person."[18] The widespread preference, among the opponents of deficit spending, for a dole rather than public works is at least partially motivated by the desire to preserve worker discipline through fear of loss of the job. By making the receipt of government disbursements as socially degrading as possible, opponents of deficit spending hope to improve the bargaining strength of private employers.

It is not likely that the "industrial reserve army" basis of opposition will soften with time. The only question is whether, should it become obvious that a reasonable degree of prosperity can be main-

[17] See, for example, statement by Representative Patman, Senate Hearings, p. 83.

[18] Letter from R. H. Thompson to Senator Robert F. Wagner, reproduced in Senate Hearings, p. 1224.

tained only by deficit spending, the self-interest of the employers may not better be served by supporting deficit spending, even though if carried very far it would adversely affect worker discipline from the point of view of the employer. Under these circumstances business men would want some deficit spending, but not too much.

Another attitude leading to opposition to full employment measures from dislike of full employment is associated with the "boom or bust" argument that we should avoid good times because they lead to bad. It is interesting to notice that the foremost theoretical economist who advocated the idea that business in the boom gets so good that it automatically becomes bad (Friedrich Hayek) is also the intellectual leader of the opposition on the basis of the fear of growing state power. The boom-or-bust argument must, however, be regarded as a rather unimportant rationalization, since few of those who hold it would be actually willing, under conditions of less than full employment, to advocate measures that would make business worse (except for the curbing of speculation), in order to prevent the boom.

V. CLASS ANTAGONISM

Closely related to the industrial reserve army basis of opposition is the belief that deficit spending, or the Full Employment Bill, is class legislation. Deficit spending is closely associated with the New Deal and the great volume of social legislation enacted since 1933. It is supported by organized labor and New Dealers. The bi-partisan support for the Full Employment Bill indicates that there was some recognition of the widespread demand for the government to take responsibility for full employment. The opposition, however, and especially the die-hard opposition, closely identified the bill with labor rather than with the economy at large.

It is hard to say to what extent opposition depended on the intrinsic features of the bill and to what extent it depended on the quarters from which the bill derived support. Some members of Congress regarded the bill as a piece of class legislation, but many others recognized the breadth of public support for a full employment bill. Among business men public support carried less weight, and the New Dealism and labor-orientation of employment legislation was probably of greater importance. Business men's resentment was intensified by the feeling that employment legislation involves a cost that falls especially sharply on them in the form of taxes. The class antagonism attitude was usually expressed by simply tarring the Full Employment Bill as a New Deal measure, but more extreme forms of attack emphasized the effects on the redistribution of income, or raised the issue of whether the government should worry about full employment while the workers were creating unemployment through strikes. Thus: "The legislation urged upon the Congress asserts that it is the 'responsibility of the Federal Government to provide such volume of Federal investment and expenditure as may be needed to assure continuing full employment.' Such pronouncement of governmental policy simply means that those who work and produce, and who consequently pay taxes and buy bonds, are to assume the responsibility to support those who fail or refuse to work and produce";[19] and: "You cannot have continuous employment if, periodically, a large number of men who are employed in a particular plant will not work."[20]

It is difficult to predict whether the class antagonism basis of opposition to government spending will weaken in the future. Class antagonisms themselves, with the new strength of labor organizations, may be expected to increase, if anything. If the opponents of deficit spending were actually successful in achieving a continuously balanced budget, one could predict that the ensuing depression, which would be inevitable unless there were a permanent upward shift in the propensity to consume, would convert many business men to the realization that some deficit spending was desirable even from their own point of view. If, as is more likely, we have enough deficit spending in the future to maintain fairly high levels of production, with unemployment no worse than in 1936–39, opposition based on class antagonism is likely to persist.

VI. FEAR OF INCREASING STATE POWER

Next to the anthropomorphic fallacy, the most frequently expressed objection to deficit spending as a cure for unemployment is that it means the end of free private enterprise. This argument was also applied against the statement in the original Full Employment Bill that it is the policy of the United States to assure employment opportunities for all. The argument was seldom carried beyond the categorical statement that government responsibility for full employment means the end of free private enterprise. Few indeed were the supporters of the bill who attempted to show that the opponents meant

[19] Senator Moore of Oklahoma, Congressional Record, 79th Congress, 1st Session, p. 9224.

[20] Representative Hoffman of Michigan, House Hearings, p. 48.

by "free private enterprise" the control of the economic system by the managerial or entrepreneurial class, or the special privileges of the owners of property; even fewer were inclined to say, "so much the worse for free enterprise." The standard reply was that another depression might really mean the end of free private enterprise, and in making the economic system work they were saving free private enterprise.

Of course the high emotional value of the term "free private enterprise" in large measure explains the frequent appeal to this principle. In recognition of this semantic value the Full Employment Bill was studded with pleasant remarks about free private enterprise, and stress was laid on the fact that the President's economic program would first attempt the greatest possible stimulation of non-Federal expenditure and investment before resorting to Federal expenditure and investment. Business spokesmen were very little impressed by these features of the bill and generally passed right by them to press their attacks on the two key points of the bill: the assumption of government responsibility for employment opportunities, and the recommendation of deficit spending as a last resort. And here they raised the cry that free private enterprise was in danger.

Was this slogan adopted because it was the most effective political weapon to implement the opposition ultimately based on the factors previously considered, or was the fear of further extension of government responsibility itself a prime motivating factor? The latter seems to be the more accurate view. This interpretation, that the fear of growing state power is a genuinely independent attitude rather than being merely a slogan used to protect other interests, has considerable inferential evidence to support it.

Most significant in this respect are the alternatives suggested to the Full Employment Bill. The most common, and certainly the most characteristic, of the proposals of the business spokesmen ran in terms of freeing business from government regulation. In particular, more favorable taxation and fewer attempts at a planned economy came highest on the list of alternative programs advanced by business men. We may, accordingly, conclude that the business man's opposition to the extension of government influence on business is really a fundamental attitude rather than one derived from the other factors we are considering.

Just how fundamental it is remains to be determined. It is clear that to a certain extent opposition to government control of business can be derived from the profit motive; the business man wants the government out of business because he can make more money that way. This applies obviously to taxation and also to social legislation which frequently is felt by the businessman to restrict his profit-making possibilities. It applied especially powerfully to wartime price and production controls.

If the principal basis of the antagonism to government responsibility for employment were derived from the profit motive, then it could reasonably be expected to weaken in the future, on the assumption that deficit spending will be necessary for the maintenance of a high enough level of production to afford a satisfactory level of profits. There is no business opposition to those governmental activities that are clearly and positively associated with profits. Protected industries do not object to tariffs as violations of free private enterprise, and legislation strengthening government regulation of trade unions would certainly be welcomed by business men in general. This is consistent with the oft-encountered statement that it is the government's task to give business a favorable climate, but not to attempt to try to run business — the "atmospheric" theory of government's relationship to business.[21]

The distinction between government as a climate-maker and government as an interferer cannot be easily drawn, but the attitude which calls for this distinction is quite understandable. The business man does not want his position as helmsman challenged. It is he, the manager or the entrepreneur, who is the decision-maker; and he does not want that position usurped by the government. What he fears from greater governmental responsibility is not the road to serfdom but the road from suzerainty. The business man does have a fear of government activity independent of the profit motive; it is the fear of government as a competitor for economic power.

This attitude is probably well founded. The business spokesmen are fond of referring to business men as job-makers, but a general acceptance of government responsibility for employment clearly implies the transfer of this title to government. The reversal of the dictum "what's good for business is good for you" to "what's good for you is good for business" forebodes a revolution in the business man's

[21] This theory was almost unanimously supported by the representatives of business men and other opponents of deficit spending and governmental responsibility. See statements of Ira Mosher, President, National Association of Manufacturers, House Hearings, p. 578; George Terborgh, Research Director, Machinery and Allied Products Institute, House Hearings, p. 602; Joseph W. Kane, representing the Chamber of Commerce, Detroit, Mich., House Hearings, p. 659; James L. Donnelly, Executive Vice-President, Illinois Manufacturers' Association, House Hearings, p. 708, to name only a few.

place in society. To a certain extent that revolution has already taken place, as is evidenced by the importance of news from Washington in the weekly "business letter." The importance of governmental decisions for business affairs has grown, relative to the importance of business men's decisions, and business interests realize this keenly. Because they do realize it so keenly, they can be expected to be particularly sensitive to the danger of further encroachment; and the explicit recognition of government responsibility for full employment represents a large-scale encroachment. Opposition was all the more stimulated by the fact that the Full Employment Bill was only a manifesto. Even if the profit motive should lead business men to accept the fact of deficit spending, it would still be politically wise for them to delay the general acceptance of the theory.

The long-run development that can be expected is the atrophy of the entrepreneurial function. The primary role of the business man, as distinct from technical management, is to adjust the operations of his business to changing economic conditions. Gradually the situation is developing wherein governmental decisions in large measure *make* these economic conditions. With this development, the government official tends to displace the business man as the key decision-maker, and, with some lag, the business man's position in society will probably be readjusted downward in keeping with his economic function. He has already descended the verbal stairs from the rank of "Industry" through "Capital" to "Management." He may in fact as well as in name become "Management" rather than "Enterprise." The business man may personally avoid this degradation by taking over the government, but even in this case the government function will in the long run come to dominate so that he will be more government official than business man.

It should be noted that the analysis above does not depend on the alleged fact that if the government should take responsibility for full employment it would have to control more and more aspects of economic life in order to discharge the obligation. It is based on a theory of social development that even if the government could insure full employment in a manner that left the maximum amount of decision-making to business men, the fact that it was the government and not the business man that was fundamentally responsible for the level of economic activity would work toward the decline of the business man and the growth of government economic activity. For there would still exist other tendencies leading to increased government economic control, the most notable being the struggle between organized labor and the business man. The government is involved in settling the struggle, and the bargaining power of the business man is impaired if it is realized that not the business man but government is determining the level of economic activity. There is a broad understanding by the general public of the impotence of the business man to stem a recession. Consequently the voters already hold the federal administration rather than the business man responsible for the level of employment.

So when a business man opposes the deficit spending theory on the grounds that it means the end of free private enterprise, he is right in that it probably does imply the decline of the free private entrepreneur. Of course, the supporters of deficit spending are also right when they say that a prolonged repetition of 1933 conditions would also mean the end of free private enterprise, and business men realize this also. It is a fair guess that they will probably go along with whatever deficit spending is required to maintain a moderately prosperous condition — say no more than the 1937 level of unemployment — but they will not accept the theory of deficit spending. This conclusion also fits in with our evaluation of the industrial reserve army basis of opposition to deficit spending considered in Section IV above.

Since the business man's fear of increasing government power as a threat to his own sovereignty is, in the writer's opinion, well founded, it may be used as an aid in explaining the continued retention of the fallacies mentioned in Section III. The business man, according to his economic sophistication, appeals to the anthropomorphic fallacy, or rejects the premise of the argument, because to do otherwise is to drive a nail into his own coffin. Furthermore, it is now clear why business spokesmen so strongly prefer emphasis on public expenditure as a dole rather than as an instrument for the prevention of unemployment. The paying of a dole by the government does not challenge the business man's position, whereas government prevention of unemployment threatens the business man's position in the economy.

VII. THE OUTLOOK

It must be admitted that when extensive unemployment is upon us deficit spending will almost certainly be undertaken to relieve it. The next recession will not be marked, as was that after 1929, by a controversy as to whether the unemployed are to be the object of private charity or public relief, but public works are likely to be speedily, though perhaps haphazardly, undertaken. These public works will most probably not involve direct government hiring of the unemployed but will be given out as contracts to private construction enterprises.[22]

The Full Employment Bill as introduced was important as a manifesto making explicit the government's responsibility for maintaining full employment. The weakened language of the final act represents a compromise between the public demand for the government's taking some responsibility and the public fear of continued increase of the national debt. It is not likely that the stronger form of the bill would have led to greater or prompter deficit spending when necessary in the future.

It is not likely that the theory of deficit spending will in the near future be embraced as an explicitly avowed policy of the Federal government, but the practice of deficit spending in depression can confidently be expected to continue. Business men's opposition to the practice may be expected to be weak under conditions of unemployment, but their opposition to explicit acceptance of the theory of deficit spending may be expected to continue. The most important single basis of opposition, and one which helps explain many of the other grounds of opposition, is the fact that government responsibility for ensuring full employment does imply a long-run decline of the importance of the business man.

---

[22] The conclusions up to this point do not follow from the preceding paper but from impressions drawn from attitudes displayed in the controversy over the Full Employment Bill.

PART FIVE

THE ROLE OF FEDERAL DEFICITS: THE EMPIRICAL RECORD

WILFRED LEWIS, JR.

Summary of Findings on Role of Fiscal Policy*

From his empirical investigation, Wilfred Lewis, Jr., concludes that built-in fiscal stabilizers have been of substantial assistance in moderating the four post-World War II recessions from 1948 to 1962, while discretionary fiscal action has been of little or no help in these periods but of some, although quite limited, aid in promoting the subsequent recoveries. In general, it appears that, in this period, the federal government, for whatever reason, did not employ a vigorous discretionary fiscal policy to combat economic contractions but relied instead, deliberately or otherwise, mainly on automatic stabilizers. For some, the results are gratifying, as the four post-World War II recessions studied were relatively mild by past standards. Others

* Abridged and reprinted by permission from *Federal Fiscal Policy in the Post-War Recessions* (Brookings Institution, Washington, 1962).

believe that more positive government fiscal action would have been warranted to still further moderate the declines and perhaps also to promote stronger recovery movements. It remains largely a matter of judgment as to how much deviation from full employment is tolerable. It is interesting to note, also, the author's view that among the constraints operating on the government was the reluctance to engage actively in deficit spending and the fear of contributing to inflation. This is contrary to a view expressed by many, including several authors in these readings, that compensatory fiscal policy would have an inflationary bias, as governments acted more vigorously to offset unemployment than inflation.

THIS study attempts to describe, measure, and evaluate the planned and unplanned fiscal actions of the federal government — changes in government receipts and expenditures — in the postwar recessions and recoveries. That the government, in theory, can counteract recession by suitably chosen fiscal policies has been demonstrated too well in a voluminous literature to require discussion here. Similarly, this study presumes agreement with, and does not undertake to defend, the general proposition that the federal government should try to use its fiscal powers to combat unemployment and promote stable growth. However, particular antirecession fiscal actions can be better or worse with respect to effectiveness, timing, efficiency, and compatibility with other goals, and some of the policies pursued in the past have been worse rather than better. It is hoped that, by examining these past actions in some detail, the choice of fiscal weapons for future recessions and the strategy used in applying them may be improved. . . .

Measuring Federal Receipts and Expenditures

A definition of fiscal activities as those involving government receipts and expenditures is not as precise as it sounds, because receipts and expenditures can be, and have been, measured in different ways. Of the alternative tabulations of federal government receipts and expenditures which have been developed over the years for various purposes, three are of central interest in studying fiscal policy:

1. *The Budget of the United States Government,* which is the focal point of the President's annual Budget Message to Congress, and — until recently — "the" budget in the parlance of most govern-

ment officials. This version is usually referred to by economists as the "administrative," "regular," or "conventional" budget.

2. *Federal Government Receipts from and Payments to the Public,* which is known to economists as the "cash" or "consolidated cash" budget. This version includes, in addition to the administrative budget transactions, such important transactions as those of the social security, unemployment, and highway trust funds, which are excluded from the administrative budget.

3. *The National Income Budget,* which reflects federal receipts and expenditures as recorded in the national income accounts of the U.S. Department of Commerce. This budget, like the consolidated cash budget, is comprehensive with respect to trust fund transactions. However, there are important differences, aimed at measuring the direct effects of federal activity on aggregate private income. Perhaps the major differences in this respect are (a) the inclusion of corporate profits taxes in the national income budget when the liability accrues, rather than when the government receives payment, and (b) the exclusion from national income account expenditures of loans, mortgage purchases, purchases of land, and similar transactions which are exchanges of existing assets rather than additions to current private incomes.[1]

The President's annual administrative budget — because it omits so many important transactions of the government and because of the timing with which it reflects others — is seriously deficient as an index of the government's impact on the economy. However, the formulation and discussion of fiscal policy by public officials traditionally has been conducted within its framework, and it will be necessary to refer to totals in the administrative budget at a number of points in this study.

The superiority of the national income tabulation of receipts and expenditures as measures of the impact of federal activity on national income is widely accepted by economists, and the focus in this analysis will be those activities summed up in the federal surplus or deficit in the national income accounts. In fact, a good definition of "fiscal" — pragmatically as well as theoretically — is in terms of those receipts and expenditures reflected in the national income accounts. Differences between the national income budget and the

---

[1] The differences between the three measures are explained in more detail in *The Budget of the United States Government for the Fiscal Year Ending June 30, 1963* (January 1962), Special Analysis B, pp. 279–82, and Special Analysis C, pp. 283–89; and in U. S. Department of Commerce, *U. S. Income and Output* (1958), Table III-10, pp. 178–79.

consolidated cash budget, for example, can almost all be reduced to differences between transactions having direct income effects on the private economy, and those which affect the supply or liquidity of assets but not directly the incomes of the private sector.[2] It is convenient to regard the former as fiscal actions, and the latter as monetary-credit-debt actions. This does not imply a difference in importance, but it does imply a difference in function. It goes without saying that no single measure of federal activity is best for all purposes. Because the national income budget deliberately excludes loans, mortgage purchases, and similar transactions in existing assets, for example, it is undoubtedly less informative for purposes of analyzing interest rates and capital markets than either the consolidated cash budget or federal transactions as recorded by the Federal Reserve in its flow-of-funds statistics. . . .

Meaning of a Budget Surplus

The use of fiscal policy to stabilize the economy calls for either increasing federal expenditures or reducing federal receipts during recessions, or both. Any of these categories of action means decreasing the surplus in the federal budget or increasing its deficit. Thus, a question naturally arises — even among those who accept the idea that the budget does not have to be balanced every fiscal year — as to what size the federal budget surplus should be "normally." And "normally" means to some an average over the business cycle, while to others it means high employment. Popular folklore about the propriety of "balanced" federal budgets to the contrary, it is not possible — at least on economic criteria — to specify in the abstract the proper absolute "normal" size of the federal surplus or deficit.

For one thing, a budget surplus or deficit of a particular size represents a greater or smaller economic impact, depending on the level and composition of the receipts and expenditures which enter into its calculation. For example, taxes are paid at least in part from private saving, without correspondingly decreasing investment, whereas government purchases of goods directly add to GNP by the full amount. Therefore, equal amounts of taxes and of government purchases will ordinarily mean that the government is adding to aggregate demand; an increase in the size of the budget will be expansionary

---

[2] See the article "Federal Receipts and Expenditures — Alternative Measures," *Monthly Review* of the Federal Reserve Bank of Kansas City, August 1961. See also Michael E. Levy, "Federal Budget: Deficit or Surplus," *Business Record* of the National Industrial Conference Board, February 1962.

even if the surplus or deficit remains unchanged.[3] However, this statement does not hold for government transfer payments,[4] since transfer payments add to GNP only indirectly — when the payments are spent by their recipients. And federal grants may cause an increase in total government spending by more than the amount included in the federal budget if states are required to put up matching funds which they otherwise would not have spent. Contrariwise, there may be little, if any, change if federal grants are substituted for amounts states would have spent from their own funds anyway.

Aside from the effects of composition, a surplus of a particular size cannot be taken as a measure of the total economic impact of government activity. Private demand will also be affected by the issuance of new government orders, federal guarantee and insurance activity, wage legislation, direct price and wage controls, monetary policy, debt management, action by regulatory agencies, and similar government activities.

Moreover, the economic effects of a surplus of any given size depend on the private response to changes in income or assets — reactions which can, and do, change over time. In short, the effects of a budget surplus of a given size will vary with its composition, with trends in federal activity which affect the economy but are not reflected in the budget, and with the strength of private income-expenditure relationships. Stated differently, a zero balance — or even a deficit at one point of time — may be no more inflationary than a surplus equal to several percentage points of GNP at another, even assuming full employment in both cases.

Since it is not possible generally to state on economic grounds the appropriate size of a federal surplus at high employment, it is fortunate that an answer to this abstract question is not really needed in order to conduct fiscal policy intelligently. Rather, the question which typically confronts the policy official is: Given the existing state of the budget, what change in budget surplus or deficit would accord with present and prospective levels of private economic activity? Economic analysis is better able to answer a question of this kind for

[3] This is the implication of the famous "balanced budget multiplier" theorem, of which the classic statement is by Trygve Haavelmo, "Multiplier Effects of a Balanced Budget," *Econometrica*, Vol. 13 (October 1945), pp. 311–18. See also Richard A. Musgrave, *The Theory of Public Finance* (McGraw-Hill, 1959), pp. 429–32.

[4] "Government transfer payments" are expenditures which add to private incomes, but for which no currently produced goods or services are rendered to the government in exchange.

two reasons: First, while determination of the precise am
impossible, the direction of the economic effect of an
expenditures or decrease in tax rates is unambiguously e:
Second, for short intervals of time, the impact of a budget surplus of a
given size often can be assumed approximately unchanged. This
follows from the facts that private income-expenditure relations and
the composition of the budget usually change slowly, and because
the unbudgeted federal activities usually also change little in the
short run.

To sum up, it is often possible to assert that, because private economic activity is falling, or is below desired levels, a decrease in the
federal surplus is called for — without even attempting to answer the
question of what absolute level of surplus or deficit would be appropriate under "normal" conditions. In other circumstances, similar reason-
ing may indicate an increase in the surplus.

THE IMPLICIT FEDERAL SURPLUS AT HYPOTHETICAL HIGH EMPLOYMENT

Because the level of national income determines the amount of
revenue collected from given tax rates, the size of the actual budget
surplus at any particular time depends passively on the level of economic activity as well as actively on discretionary tax and expenditure
actions. In using the budget surplus to indicate whether discretionary
fiscal behavior has neutral, expansionary, or contractionary effects on
the economy, it is essential to distinguish between active and passive
changes in the surplus. The distinction is made at several places in
this study by the use of an analytical tool of fairly recent development
— the implicit federal surplus.

The implicit federal surplus, as used in this study, is the difference between federal receipts and expenditures calculated for existing
programs and tax rates, but assuming the economy is at high employment so far as the fiscal effects of the built-in stabilizers are concerned.
The basic idea underlying this concept of implicit federal surplus is
not new. It bears a close kinship, for example, to the "stabilizing
budget" policy which has been recommended by the Committee for
Economic Development (CED) since early in the postwar period.[5]
The CED's suggested policy would set discretionary taxes and expenditures so as to yield some surplus at high employment and would
tolerate deficits caused by induced declines in tax collections if eco-

[5] See *Taxes and the Budget* (Committee for Economic Development, 1947).

nomic activity fell below high employment. However, until recently there have been few attempts to draw fiscal policy conclusions or recommendations from quantitative estimates or judgments about the size of the federal surplus at hypothetical high employment.[6]

If a decrease in the *actual* federal surplus in recession represents nothing more than the automatic drop in revenues or increase in unemployment compensation caused by the drop in economic activity below a high employment trend, the *implicit* federal surplus will remain unchanged in size. With tax rates and government expenditure programs unchanged, fiscal policy can be regarded as neutral in an important sense, rather than compensatory or expansionary. This does not mean that the income-generating effects of a deficit caused by built-in stabilizers are any less than if the deficit were the result of discretionary factors. Rather, it refers to the fact that a purely passive federal offset to private expenditure reductions would be self-reversing with the start of recovery and self-terminating with the return of the economy to high employment. A budget policy which is neutral in this sense is consistent with a return to high employment and recovery of the pre-existing rate of utilization of other factors of production only if the original cause of decline in private spending is removed, or if it is offset by increases in other categories of private spending.[7] A decrease in the size of the implicit federal surplus, on the other hand, can be taken as indicating that the income-generating effects of the budget have increased relative to high employment GNP.

A neutral budget policy can be successful only if the recession is caused by a temporary and self-correcting decline of private expenditures. Even more important, unless fiscal policy makes use of calculations on a fairly current basis of the size and effects of the implicit surplus, there is danger of perverse fiscal behavior which would aggravate the decline in private spending — or, more likely, slow or prevent complete recovery. This is because actual figures on the budget surplus may give misleading signals during recession about the income-generating effects of the budget. The passive drop in revenues

---

[6] See statement of Charles L. Schultze in *Current Economic Situation and Outlook*, Joint Economic Committee Hearings, 86 Cong. 2 sess. (1961), pp. 120–22; statement of Herbert Stein in *Hearings on the Economic Report of the President*, Joint Economic Committee, 87 Cong. 1 sess. (1961), pp. 209 ff.; and CEA, *Economic Report of the President, January 1962*, pp. 79–84.

[7] "Neutral" in this sense can be viewed as short-run neutrality. In the long run, the degree of built-in flexibility in the budget must be viewed as a variable which can be changed as a matter of public policy.

can produce a decrease in actual surplus large enough to hide an increase in the implicit surplus.

The foregoing possibilities are not idle speculations. The record of discretionary fiscal policy during the postwar recessions and recoveries has left something to be desired. And misleading budget signals given off by actual, rather than implicit, surpluses and deficits are a part of this story. . . .

THE FINDINGS IN BRIEF

Since the major focus of this study is on fiscal policy, much attention is given to distinguishing among and, to the extent possible, determining separate amounts involved in automatic built-in fiscal stabilizers, discretionary antirecessionary actions, and expenditure and tax changes occurring primarily for reasons other than recessions. An overall summary of federal receipts and expenditures during the four postwar recessions and recoveries, as shown in Table 4, provides a useful point of departure.

Automatic Stabilizers

The built-in fiscal stabilizers have made a substantial contribution to the stability of the postwar economy. They have pushed the federal budget strongly toward deficit when that was needed in each postwar recession, thus helping to slow the economic decline. The resulting change in the surplus has been large relative to the change in total output, ranging from 40 percent of the fall in GNP from peak to trough in 1948–50 to more than 100 percent in 1960–61. Moreover, in spite of a lagged impact on the federal cash budget, the economic effects of the built-in stabilizers have been timely with respect to contraction. It appears likely that the built-in stabilizers have limited the duration as well as the severity of postwar contractions. Of course, after the trough is passed and employment and output rise, the built-in stabilizers reverse direction. Then they increase the surplus or reduce the deficit, and thus retard recovery.

The built-in fiscal stabilizers are of two general types: some have direct effects; others, indirect effects. Those having a direct effect on disposable personal income — individual income tax, unemployment compensation, and employment taxes — have become somewhat more important for several reasons. Increases in payroll tax rates, mainly for old-age and survivors insurance (OASI), have so promoted employment taxes as a built-in stabilizer that their effects on government

TABLE 4 — SUMMARY OF FEDERAL RECEIPTS AND EXPENDITURES, POST-WAR RECESSIONS AND RECOVERIES[1]

(In billions of current dollars)

Recession and recovery	Peak quarter	Trough quarter	Terminal quarter of recovery	Change, peak to trough	Change, trough to recovery
1948–50	1948-IV	1949-II	1950-II		
Receipts	42.6	38.5	47.3	−4.1	8.8
Expenditures	38.8	42.4	39.0	3.6	−3.4
Surplus or deficit(−)	3.8	−3.9	8.3	−7.7	12.2
(Change in surplus due to built-in fiscal stabilizers)	....	....	....	(−3.7)	(6.1)
1953–55	1953-II	1954-II	1955-II		
Receipts	72.3	63.3	71.7	−9.0	8.4
Expenditures	79.4	68.7	68.1	−10.7	−0.6
Surplus or deficit(−)	−7.0	−5.4	3.5	1.6	8.9
(Change in surplus due to built-in fiscal stabilizers)	....	....	....	(−6.6)	(10.4)
1957–59	1957-III	1958-I	1959-II		
Receipts	82.5	75.4	91.6	−7.1	16.2
Expenditures	79.9	83.5	91.1	3.6	7.6
Surplus or deficit(−)	2.6	−8.1	0.5	−10.7	8.6
(Change in surplus due to built-in fiscal stabilizers)	....	....	....	(−8.7)	(17.4)
1960–61	1960-II	1961-I	1961-IV[2]		
Receipts	96.9	92.5	103.1	−4.4	10.6
Expenditures	92.5	98.0	105.2	5.5	7.2
Surplus or deficit(−)	4.5	−5.5	−2.1	−10.0	3.4
(Change in surplus due to built-in fiscal stabilizers)	....	....	....	(−6.8)	(10.8)

1 On basis of national income accounts, seasonally adjusted annual rates. From Table 5 and U. S. Department of Commerce, *U. S. Income and Output* (1958) and *Survey of Current Business,* July 1961 and February 1962. Figures here and in subsequent tables may not add because of rounding.

2 The last quarter for which data are available is 1961-IV, although 1962-II is considered the terminal quarter of recovery in this study.

receipts are now about a third as large as the variations in the yield of the individual income tax. At unchanged tax rates, the individual income tax grows faster than gross national product and seems to have acquired somewhat increased sensitivity to cyclical changes in GNP. Finally, there is some evidence that private consumption has become more responsive to cyclical changes in disposable personal income, and this promotes the importance of the stabilizers which directly cushion declines in such income.

The indirect stabilizers — corporation income tax and excises — account for larger portions of the change in federal surplus or deficit than the direct stabilizers. However, at least for minor recessions, they are inefficient because they probably add substantially less to private spending than they subtract from federal budget receipts. This effect might be a net disadvantage if the public and political response were so opposed to budget deficits that expansionary fiscal action of a discretionary nature were thereby inhibited. Moreover, concern about budget deficits is strengthened by the lag in the collection of corporation income taxes, which produces a cash budget deficit after recovery is under way.

Discretionary Fiscal Actions

... Compared to the automatic stabilizers, deliberate actions to counter recessions generally have been less helpful. Recession is never the only factor, and seldom the most important factor, shaping federal fiscal and budgetary policy. As a consequence, specific antirecession actions have been subject to numerous constraints which have limited their effectiveness from a stabilization standpoint.

As a rule, the government has favored countercyclical actions that could be justified, at least in part, on other than purely stabilization grounds. This is perhaps the major reason why countercyclical actions on the expenditure side of the budget have had more appeal than tax cuts, which would have required justification primarily on counterrecession grounds. Under this "mixed motives" approach, expenditures which would have been undertaken anyway sometimes have been labeled "counterrecession." The converse is probably also true — some redefinition of long-term program goals undoubtedly has taken place in the heat of battle against recession. As a consequence, it is frequently difficult — sometimes impossible — to decide definitely whether or not the motive in particular actions was primarily to counter recession. But, insofar as a distinction is possible, those actions which appear to have been primarily counterrecessionary have been on the expenditure side of the budget. A possible exception is the reduction of excise taxes in 1954, for which the recession was a frequently advanced but not the only argument.

Measured by changes in the implicit federal surplus at high employment during the recession phase, discretionary fiscal actions of the federal government were sharply contractionary during the recession of 1953–54, were mildly expansionary in 1948–49, and were approximately neutral during the other recessions. The story during the recovery phases is less favorable, even allowing for discretionary antirecession actions. In the 1949–50 and 1954–55 recoveries, the implicit surplus increased even though the economy was still below high employment. In both these cases, however, a net increase in the implicit surplus in the terminal quarter compared to the prerecession peak proved not to be too restrictive a budget policy in the light of later developments in the economy. In the 1958–59 recovery, the implicit surplus through the end of calendar 1959 was not much larger than it had been before the recession. However, a reaction to the very large fiscal 1959 deficit resulted in cutbacks in expenditures which, coupled with tax increases, caused a drastic increase in the rate of the implicit federal surplus in early 1960. The 1960–62 period of recession and recovery is the only one for which the implicit surplus declined from prerecession peak to terminal quarter (based on expectations in March 1962). However, the prospect in early 1962 was for a reversal of this behavior by the end of the year and prior to the achievement of what the administration had declared was its full employment target of 4 percent unemployed.

Interestingly, the general magnitude of counterrecessionary increases in expenditures has been roughly the same for the three recessions in which such actions took place, in spite of different mixtures of actions. . . . The 1954 recession featured an administrative speed-up which leaned heavily on the Department of Defense. In 1958, Congress was considerably more aggressive, but the administrative speed-up that year exempted the Department of Defense. The 1961 administrative actions included activities of the Department of Defense, and featured congressional action also, but less than in 1958. Although the President proposed some steps in 1949, no significant counterrecession actions were actually undertaken in that recession.

A direct comparison of the relative contributions of deliberate counterrecession actions and built-in stabilizers is somewhat misleading because of different timing. Discretionary actions have not been in effect before the trough month so that, except for possible anticipatory effects, they have not been a factor in cushioning the decline or in causing turning points. On the other hand, discretionary actions have made a contribution during the recovery phase, which is a time when the built-in stabilizers reverse direction and operate to slow recovery. However, the fiscal effects (and reasonable estimates of economic effects) of discretionary actions during the recovery phase have been considerably smaller than the contribution of the automatic stabilizers during the recession phase.

It has not been difficult to reverse discretionary actions, at least for those identified as primarily counterrecessionary. Such actions generally have been self-terminating, or were terminated by discretionary action prior to full recovery. Actions that might be more difficult to reverse, such as new public works starts (as distinguished from speeding work in progress) generally have been avoided.

While expenditures could be, and were, justified in part on other than stabilization grounds, tax cuts would have required (or at least were so viewed) an admission by public officials that a recession was serious enough to call for corrective action not otherwise justifiable. This made the expenditure side more attractive to public officials, particularly in the early stages of recession when the extent of need for corrective action was still uncertain. In addition, tax cuts faced a serious obstacle on those occasions when they were considered or recommended because they involved controversial questions of equity and the distribution of tax burdens by income groups.

Constraints on Antirecession Policy

Some of the constraints under which discretionary actions have operated recur with enough frequency to command more attention than they generally get from economic analysts.

A major category of constraints on counterrecession policy can be described as "prior commitments and long-range goals." It would have been most difficult for President Truman, just re-elected in a campaign featuring charges of Republican "fiscal irresponsibility" for having cut taxes in 1948, to have proposed tax cuts in January 1949. Similarly, it would have been difficult for the newly installed Eisenhower administration, pledged to reduce spending and the budget deficit, to propose expenditure increases in 1953–54; or for newly elected President Kennedy, having pledged expenditure increases and possibly tax increases to meet the Soviet threat, to ask for tax cuts in 1961. Such commitments are not necessarily inconsistent with counterrecession action, but certainly limit the range of policy alternatives.

Short-run uncertainty about whether the economy was or was not in recession, or about to be in recession, has been a limitation on counterrecession action, but not so serious as public statements and appearances might suggest. Concern over the need to maintain public and business confidence has sometimes limited public acknowledgment of recession and delayed the initiation of corrective actions. As a rule, administrations have delayed public acknowledgment of recession until the evidence was overwhelming — well into the period of decline — but have called the turn promptly, and started to reimpose fiscal restraints, as soon as the trough was passed and recovery started. Uncertainty about whether the economy might not a year or so hence be faced with the problem of inflation has been a greater limitation than inability to make short-term forecasts. Lack of certainty about the government's own requirements for defense expenditures has been a factor in this. In at least three of the four postwar recessions, there were, at times which were critical for purposes of antirecession decisions, strong feelings that defense expenditures might have to be increased by unknown, but potentially inflationary, amounts. As a consequence, there has been a high — probably too high — premium on reversibility, and often actions that were judged not reversible were avoided. The feeling that tax cuts might prove irreversible, for example, was a definite factor against their use.

Concern over balanced budgets in one form or another has been an active constraint in each postwar recession. There have been only brief interludes around the trough when the desire for balanced budgets has been suspended temporarily in favor of deliberate additions to the budget deficits. The 1946 Employment Act probably stimulated more aggressive antirecession actions than might otherwise have been forthcoming. However, there is little in the record to support the contention sometimes voiced that this legislation has biased public policy toward inflation by promoting more aggressive action to combat unemployment than inflation. Sentiments for balanced budgets and fiscal responsibility are still strong; discretionary antirecession actions have been reversed sharply during recovery. And it can be argued that any strengthening by the Employment Act of the linkage in public attitudes between the budget and the state of the economy applies to inflation as well as unemployment. Neither major party has shown a monopoly on "fiscal responsibility," and it has not been the exclusive property of either the executive or legislative branches. Anxiety over rising prices during some of the contractions and some of the recoveries has also operated as a constraint on expansionary fiscal actions, and balance of payments difficulties also played this role at the time of the 1959 recovery and the 1960–62 recession and recovery.

Recurring attention to the geographical distribution of expenditures by surplus labor areas has not enhanced overall stabilization goals, and the attention given to such attempts may have delayed action on other more effective measures. There have also been repeated suggestions to raise minimum wages — an ambiguous antirecession action at best.

Concern with "efficiency" aspects of budgeting by both the executive branch and Congress has sometimes served as a constraint on counterrecession expenditures. For example, the Department of Defense was left out of the 1958 procurement speed-up partly because it was felt that this was inconsistent with program objectives. In 1961, when consideration was being given to a list of public works projects which agencies could start within six months and complete within two years if additional funds became available, the point was made that several of the projects on the list were needed less than other larger and slower projects. Further, the starting of additional military public works for purely counterrecession purposes was questioned as possibly inconsistent with defense goals.

Other constraints have been present in the principle of trust fund financing and earmarked revenues for highways, social security, and unemployment. There is evidence that expenditures for highways have more potential flexibility than most other federally financed public works. However, under present arrangements, highway expenditures are closely geared to earmarked highway-user charges, so that any speed-up requires offsetting increases of tax rates immediately or within a short period. (In 1958, highway expenditures were accelerated, but the condition of the trust fund at that time was fortuitous and temporary.) This forestalled using highways as an antirecession action in 1961. Similarly, social security and unemployment expenditure proposals often have had to be matched by early payroll tax rate increases, the timing of which has not been helpful from a stabilization standpoint. There has been at least one increase in OASI payroll tax rates — in support of the trust fund principle — in each of the four recession-recovery periods.

Considering their timing and generally modest proportions, it seems doubtful that the discretionary counterrecession actions can be assigned much importance in limiting the duration or severity of the postwar recessions. The fact that accomplishments were as great as they were suggests that equity, national needs, or other arguments than recession could be marshalled in behalf of the actions that were taken.

Given the many constraints that have been operative, and the general absence of detailed contingency plans, it is somewhat problematical whether fiscal programs which were more expansionary could have been put together on short notice if, in fact, they had been needed. The variety of *ad hoc* expenditure proposals, and the ingenuity with which these were defended, suggest that the government may have come close to reaching the full potential of the flexibility that exists on the expenditure side of the budget. Also, the political sensitivity of equity aspects of tax cuts, and the failure to reach advance political consensus on which tax cuts would have been most desirable in recession, make it unlikely that quick action could have been taken on the tax side.

Federal fiscal actions, undertaken primarily for reasons other than the recession, on some occasions have been perverse; on other occasions, they have been more helpful in stimulating the economy than actions taken primarily to counter recession. Drastic tightening of federal fiscal activity for budgetary reasons or long-run program goals was a major initiating factor in the 1953–54 and the 1960–61 recessions, and an aggravating factor during the early stages of the 1957–58 decline. A large well-timed tax cut in 1948 helped greatly to cushion the 1948–49 decline, but was undertaken for quite different reasons. Increases in defense outlays at one stage or another of the 1949, 1958, and 1961 recessions were fortuitous since they reduced the need for discretionary counterrecession actions that might not so easily have won approval.

By concentrating on the effectiveness or ineffectiveness of particular fiscal proposals and actions, and on cataloging the constraints which have operated on public officials, it is hoped that this study will help to define the policy problems which are likely to be faced in future recessions. However, this approach makes it easy to lose sight of the real progress that has been made over the postwar period in improving the fiscal response to recession. In 1948–49, both the Congress and the executive branch initially had appeared so opposed to unbalanced budgets as to pose a threat of quite perverse fiscal actions. By the middle of 1949, at least a passive budget deficit was accepted and even defended by President Truman as the proper policy. In 1954, President Eisenhower's administration was willing to accept a limited number of discretionary increases in public spending. By 1958, Congress and Eisenhower's second administration both undertook a wide range of antirecession actions, although with some reluctance on the part of the administration and some regret on the part of both branches afterwards. And in 1961, the Kennedy administration proposed promptly and publicly a coordinated attack on recession — still, however, with signs of regret about the deficit financing this entailed, and a rather hasty reversal after the initiation of recovery was assured.

There are many remaining constraints, however, and a great deal of work is needed to sharpen the fiscal tools to be used in combating recession, and in improving the skill and timing with which they are used. It is especially important that the deficits generated automatically during recession shall not be allowed to provoke fiscal reactions that impede the return of the economy to high employment.

CONCLUSION

There is at present near unanimity among economists on the view that fiscal policy in general and budget deficits in particular can be helpful in promoting prosperity. This has become the new fiscal orthodoxy. The opposite view, recommending adherence to the classical orthodoxy of balanced budgets, as represented in these readings by the position of the National Association of Manufacturers, receives little support; and, as Sidney Alexander suggests, such support for this view as does exist rests primarily on political rather than economic considerations.

Lerner presents a cogent case for compensatory fiscal policy or, in his terms, functional finance; his article does, however, unduly minimize the complexities that must be dealt with in the execution of such a policy. Most students of the subject are not quite as optimistic as Lerner and incorporate in their analyses more emphasis on conflicts in goals and shortcomings which impair the effectiveness of any fiscal program. These include problems of prediction, timing, legislative delay, possible inflationary bias, and others. Some, including Colm and Heller, while recognizing the difficulties, nevertheless conclude that the potential gains from discretionary fiscal policy far outweigh the costs and risks. Others, such as the Committee for Economic Development, disagree and argue instead for the more conservative policy of reliance on automatic built-in fiscal stabilizers. In spite of such differences in emphasis, we do find a high degree of agreement among economists that judicious use of fiscal policy can contribute materially to economic stability and prosperity, but not, at least with our present institutions and knowledge, to uninterrupted prosperity together with stable prices. This general conclusion is confirmed in these readings by Gerhard Colm in his analysis of our experience from 1933 to 1951 and by Wilfred Lewis, Jr., in his empirical investigation of the performance of federal fiscal policy from 1948 to 1962.

94216

SUGGESTIONS FOR ADDITIONAL READING

Alvin H. Hansen, a leading exponent of the use of fiscal policy as a device for stabilization and growth, has written widely on the subject. His pioneering efforts in the field can be found in *Fiscal Policy and Business Cycles* (Norton, New York, 1941). This book emphasizes the use of fiscal policy to combat depression and secular stagnation. In a later work, *Economic Policy and Full Employment* (McGraw-Hill, New York, 1947), Hansen stresses the fact that fiscal policy is a tool which can and should be utilized to fight inflation as well as depression. A defense of deficit spending together with an interesting attempt to measure the effects of budget deficits in the decade of the 1930's can be found in Henry H. Villard, *Deficit Spending and the National Income* (Farrar and Rinehart, New York, 1941). William H. Beveridge in his book, *Full Employment in a Free Society* (Norton, New York, 1945), strongly supports the use of fiscal policy for stabilization purposes but also suggests the need for other policies, including some direct control of private investment. Walter P. Egle in *Economic Stabilization—Objectives, Rules and Mechanisms* (Princeton University Press, Princeton, N. J., 1952) distinguishes between the use of fiscal and other stabilization policies to combat secular stagnation, which was a prime concern of Hansen in his early writings on the subject, and its use to correct short-run fluctuations. Paul J. Strayer in *Fiscal Policy and Politics* (Harper, New York, 1958) contends that, to a considerable degree, the implementation of appropriate fiscal policy to help achieve healthy and stable prosperity has been hampered by political factors such as conflicts among special interest groups, government delay, and lack of leadership. An account of the history and changing views on the role of fiscal policy can be found in Lewis H. Kimmel's *Federal Budget and Fiscal Policy, 1789–1958* (The Brookings Institution, Washington, D. C., 1959). Two recent books which contain an analysis of fiscal policy in conjunction with the political considerations involved in the post-World War II period are A. E. Holman, *United States Fiscal Policy, 1945–1959* (Oxford University Press, London, 1961), and Wilfred Lewis, Jr., *Federal Fiscal Policy in the Postwar Recessions* (The Brookings Institution, Washington, D. C., 1962). An excerpt from the latter book is included in these readings.